Praise for *How to Create*

"This book is jam-packed with creative and practical tools to help enhance your homeschooling journey and keep the love of learning alive in your child from day one until graduation!"
— Sheila Jones, Executive Director, Homeschool Alliances, Grand Canyon University

"As a child development specialist, I have always believed that educating children begins with educating the adults in their lives. Dr. Lyle Lee Jenkins and Kelly Hawkinson Lippert have written THE book that every parent must read as they prepare to educate their children at home. This in-depth model will provide parents with the essential tools needed for guiding children on their journey to become lifelong learners."
— Kathy Eggers, Author of *The Homegrown Preschooler, A Year of Playing Skillfully, A Summer of Playing Skillfully, 101 Easy Wacky Crazy Activities,* and *Solutions for Early Childhood Directors*

"Too often in our home-school culture, we are driven by fear and traditional systems of teaching. In *How to Create a Perfect Home School,* Dr. Lyle Lee Jenkins and Kelly Hawkinson Lippert brilliantly offer insights and practical resources to help shift the home education experience from a fear-based program to an environment that inspires a long-term will and thrill to learn. Every home educator needs this field guide for cultivating and maintaining the intrinsic love of learning our kids were born with."
— Amy Davis, Home Educator and CEO, Davis and Co.

"As a former home-school mom who educated my children through high school, I wish I had had this book then. One of the things I struggled with was confidence. I constantly doubted myself and my ability to teach my children with excellence. Dr. Jenkins and Kelly Hawkinson Lippert give homeschoolers confidence in their abilities. This is a wonderful book."

— Rita Hudgens, Transform University Founder,
Mental Strength Coach, Speaker and Trainer

How to
Create a Perfect
Home School

Mark,

Your support for this work with children & parents is so much appreciated! Thanks!

Jess Gard

So appreciate your support!

Kelly Lint

How to Create a Perfect Home School is written with two voices. Lyle Lee Jenkins wrote the "how to" and Kelly Hawkinson Lippert wrote the "what happened."

This combination of instruction and stories makes for a delightful, honest experience. Kelly's writing is separated from Lyle Lee's with spacing and is shown in bold italics.

How to Create a Perfect Home School

Building Confidence for Home Educators

Lyle Lee Jenkins and Kelly Hawkinson Lippert

Foreword by Mark Victor Hansen

ISBN: 978-1-956457-49-0 (paperback)
ISBN: 978-1-956457-50-6 (ebook)

Book design: Christy Day, Constellation Book Services
e-book design: Maggie McLaughlin
Publishing Consultant: Martha Bullen, Bullen Publishing Services
Editor: Darren Barakat
Photographer for Cover: Jessica Juniper
Graphics (figures and appendices): Christy Courtright, Christy's Customs

Printed in the United States of America

Further Support for Home and Classroom Educators located on Amazon under Lyle Lee Jenkins:

Bible Patterns for Young Readers Series
Aesop Patterns for Young Readers Series
How to Create Math Experts Series
How to Create Bible Experts: Genesis to Revelation
How to Create Language Experts with Literary Terms
Wordless Books for Young Authors Series
My Custom Dictionary

All pages in the appendices may be downloaded as PDFs with the QR Code

Lyle Lee Jenkins dedicates this book to Sandra Baxter Jenkins
1943-2021

Pictures of her with Bill Martin Jr. are below.

Kelly Hawkinson Lippert dedicates
this book to her three children...

It's in the trenches of life with these three humans that
I discover what it means to be a mom and a home educator.
Without them this book wouldn't exist.

CONTENTS

LIST OF FIGURES FOR HOME SCHOOL

ACKNOWLEDGEMENTS

Lyle Lee acknowledges the significant learning given to him over his career in public education. Each of the people Lyle Lee considers mentors—Evelyn Neufeld, Peggy McLean, Mary Laycock, Marion Nordberg, Bill Martin Jr., Vic Cottrell, and John Hattie—began their career as a classroom teacher.. W. Edwards Deming provided major learning for me as a teacher of adults.

Over the past 20 years Lyle Lee, as a speaker and consultant, has worked with public schools, charter schools, Christian schools (Catholic and Protestant) and now home schools. The children in each of these settings are equally precious, and Lyle Lee is so thankful for all the additional practical advice from teachers and administrators in each environment.

Without Kelly Hawkinson Lippert's eagerness to be the very best teacher for her three children, this book would not exist. She is an avid learner whose insightful writing will inspire thousands of home educators.

Books require a lot of behind the scenes help and Lyle Lee and Kelly acknowledge that without wonderful assistance from so many, this book would not exist. Darren Barakat sees more details than should be humanly possible, but his editing is greatly appreciated. Christy Courtright has created all of the figures and the appendix. Jessica Juniper created the photograph for the cover. We never imagined the setting like this for the cover photo. Impressive! At the center of advice is Martha Bullen, whose wisdom with all major decisions is loved. Christy Day takes the figures and our words and places them into a book that is laid out in an accessible, beautiful manner. The last step is for Maggie McLaughlin to place the book on Amazon for print and e-book and with Ingram for wholesale purchases.

We relied upon advice from Allen Jenkins, Jim Chansler, and Jeff Burgard for advice in science and the arts. Their key points were the foundation for a whole chapter.

Whew! We are grateful!

FOREWORD

Creating a perfect home school is easy if you just know how to do it. My friends Lyle Lee and Kelly have done it and made it step-by-step easy for you to apprehend, comprehend, and implement. You will become great and inspiring homeschoolers.

Everyone wise wants a superior lifelong educational experience, and homeschooling has become the new standard of can-do excellence led by family members who really love, care for, and want the absolute best for their children.

The central theme of Jenkins and Lippert's *How to Create a Perfect Home School* is skill, will, and thrill. They prove how home-school students can surpass society's skill expectations, maintain their will to work hard, and receive great thrill from the learning.

This book includes two voices: Lyle Lee explains the "how to" for success with skill, will, and thrill. Kelly describes the practical application and results utilizing Lyle Lee's learning strategies with her own children. Lyle Lee draws on the education wisdom gained from 50 years of being mentored by world-class educators. Kelly implements the concepts with her two boys as her 3-year-old daughter observes and soaks it all up. *How to Create a Perfect Home School* is theory into practice at its very best.

Jenkins and Lippert's aim for the book is to give home educators the necessary confidence to become expert teachers without purchasing a page-by-page packaged program. A master craftsman is familiar with the tools and knows precisely how to use them.

Implementation of the relevant and practical advice by Jenkins and Lippert will cause readers to become education experts surrounded by exemplary tools. They will have the ears to listen to the learning desires of their children and know exactly what assignment to provide at any given time.

The book moves through deep dives into reading, writing, and math followed by chapters on history, geography, language arts, music, art, science, and then the climax chapter on the Bible. I believe we have entered a historical time when everyone needs to know the Bible story better than ever. Bible study at home will advance children's minds and remind parents of the great moral and ethical truths that have withstood the test of time.

Prepare to enjoy and experience the skill, will, and thrill beyond your expectations as hardworking kids learn to love the joy of lifelong learning.

Mark Victor Hansen
Co-author of the *Chicken Soup for the Soul series* and co-author of *Ask! The Bridge from Your Dreams to Your Destiny* with Crystal Dwyer Hansen

Introduction

A school superintendent asked a home educator why she homeschooled. The reply was, "I can keep my children interested in learning all the way through high school, and you cannot." The superintendent had to agree that his system did not keep most of the students interested in learning. We applaud the parent's answer, but the reality is not all home-school students maintain their kindergarten love of learning, and not all public-school students lose their love of learning.

In a prior book, *How to Create a Perfect School*, Lyle Lee outlines how public, private, and charter schools can greatly increase the number of students who maintain their kindergarten desire to learn. Any structure, including home school, can destroy this intrinsic love of learning. Conversely, all school structures can be organized to maintain an intrinsic love of learning.

Home educators have the most control over the maintenance of the intrinsic motivation their children received at birth. Just like schools cannot buy intrinsic motivation, neither can home educators. It is not for sale. It is a mind-set that readers will learn throughout the pages of *How to Create a Perfect Home School*.

Home educators are intrinsically motivated to teach their own children. When people are intrinsically motivated, they work really hard, and they love the work (most days). Parents want this intrinsic motivation to be present within their children. Parents want them to work hard in school and to love the learning. In this book, we will refer to these motivation terms as "will and thrill." *How to Create a Perfect Home School* will describe the mind-set that has will and thrill continually in focus and how to measure both.

The triplets of skill, will, and thrill come from John Hattie, author of *Visible Learning*, *Visible Learning for Parents*, and many other books for educators. Readers will learn that the method for measuring skill has much influence upon the maintenance of will and thrill. Think of skill measurement as a baseball bat. It can be used for harm or for joy. Far too often, skill measurement seems to the children like they have been hit over the head with a baseball bat. Of course, they become discouraged, with will and thrill taking a nosedive. Home school can and will do far better.

Utilizing measurement of skill as an instrument for great joy is simple, but it is unique in the world of both traditional schools and home schools.

The word "perfect" is in the book title for a specific reason. First, no education system, traditional or home school, is perfect. Nevertheless, having a definition of perfect in any organization is one of the best tools to attain excellence. Once the definition of perfect is agreed upon, steps can be taken to move closer and closer to perfect. Without the definition of perfect, many organizations flounder, responding to the latest fad. This certainly is true in the world of education. We define "perfect" as maintaining intrinsic motivation to learn all the way from kindergarten until the students launch from home and go off to college or other pursuits. The reason this is so important is that there is no limit to what young people who still have this inborn, God-given, intrinsic motivation to learn can accomplish. When the will and thrill disappear and students no longer care about learning the skill, schooling becomes a huge struggle.

Readers of *How to Create a Perfect Home School* will increase the strategies by adding to those described herein. That is wonderful. Keep it up as we move forward together.

Lyle Lee Jenkins

Kelly Hawkinson Lippert

Scottsdale, Arizona

LtoJPress.com

CHAPTER 1

The Big Why

"People are asking for better schools with no clear idea of how to improve education, nor even how to define improvement of education."

W. Edwards Deming

"Perfect" in education is defined as a system where students maintain the natural intrinsic motivation to learn that arrived with them at birth. In *How to Create a Perfect Home School*, home educators will learn how this can become their reality. The will to work hard to learn and the thrill from the learning can and will be maintained all through the home-school experience. This does not mean that there won't be bad days, but these are overcome, and the overall love of learning will not be destroyed.

As a former public-school educator who is now homeschooling my own children, I have to be honest that I got discouraged with bad days at first. I felt like maybe I was doing a disservice to my children. I have come to find out that bad days look and feel different when it is my own children because of the comfort they have with me. I'm grateful, now, that they don't have to hold in their frustration all day and that we can work through it together when they're feeling it. They're allowed to process all their emotions on the spot and given grace and extra time if needed. Because of this, they are able to maintain their enthusiasm for learning much more than they ever would in a school setting. They never get left behind.

In *How to Create a Perfect School*, I reported my research on the loss of intrinsic motivation. John Hattie, author of *Visible Learning*, labeled the research "The Jenkins Curve." He shares it widely in his many worldwide seminars for educators. I conducted the research by asking 3,000 teachers who were attending one of my seminars a question: "What grade level do you teach, and what percentage of your students love school?" The result was shocking.

Prior to this research, I had assumed that elementary schools kept enthusiasm high, and it was lost in middle school and high school. That's not true. The loss begins in kindergarten and continues in every grade level until there is a low of 37% who love school in grade 9.

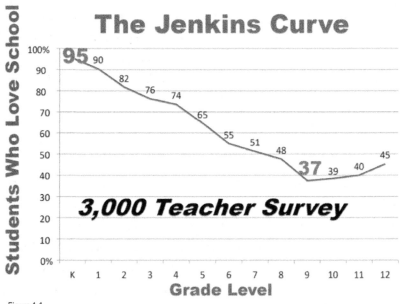

Figure 1.1

Teachers are not discouraging students on purpose. They are caught up in a culture that says you work hard doing something that is not very enjoyable, then as a reward for your hard work we give you more free time, more recess time, or a treasure jar. False dichotomy means people must choose between two things; they cannot have both at the same time. Learning and joy is a false dichotomy; both are simultaneously possible. Maintaining joy and excellence in learning is the BIG why of this book. Culture also promotes another false dichotomy: You can follow what Jesus Christ desires for your life, or you can have fun. Both are not possible. Together we will destroy both false dichotomies.

Learning is one of the most enjoyable aspects of life. When learning assignments create continual pain, it is time to rethink the method being used. Usually, it is not what the adult wants the children to learn that is a bad idea. The problem is the method utilized for the children to learn the content. For example, parents want their children to learn to read well. The most common method for learning to read is phonics. It works for many children, but not for all. If the method, phonics, is not working, find another method. The reading aim is appropriate, but often the method needs to be adjusted.

One of the biggest joys I have with homeschooling my children is the joy they're getting out of learning things they want. My second-grade son is learning about all the states and where they are located. This is because he wanted to. He is constantly striving to learn more, so he practices with his United States puzzle and blank maps so that he will improve on his quizzes each week. This is a goal he set entirely on his own. If it were up to me, I would have waited to teach this when he was in fifth grade because that's what I did at the public school. I'm so grateful I have been learning to adjust my expectations and methods of teaching because my children never cease to surprise me. Over and over, it has been proven that their desire to learn allows them to learn infinitely more than they would if I had forced them to learn the way I wanted them to.

Many readers have an elevator speech. It is an answer to the question, "What do you do for a living?" It is so short that it can be answered on the short trip on an elevator. One answer to the question, "Lee, what do you do for a living?" is "I show adults how to keep children's natural love of learning alive and well." If the conversation continues beyond the elevator, I can explain how I maintain the love of learning children possess at birth and accelerate learning beyond our wildest dreams. My desire is for "The Jenkins Curve" to land in history in education books.

I believe in what Dr. Jenkins does wholeheartedly. School has drastically changed for us in all the best ways because we have implemented his strategies and used his knowledge to strive for the perfect home school. However, it must be said that we are all humans. Humans have emotions, bad days, great days, easy days, and hard days. We decided that homeschooling was the best route for our family. We work through the challenges not because it's easy, but because it is worth it. One of the most important takeaways from my experience in implementing Dr. Jenkins' strategies is that my idea of what school looks like needed to change. I can't count workbook pages or how many things on my to-do list that I checked off. I also can't add up how many hours we spend at the table "doing work." School is more than that. School isn't "getting done" with anything. It's acquiring knowledge and making connections. That doesn't always happen in the time or manner that we have all been accustomed to, and that's okay. We are learning and growing with our children, and that is the beautiful thing about homeschooling.

"When I found my why, I found my wings." John C. Maxwell, *Good Leaders Ask Great Questions, Chart House, New York, 2014, page 35.*

CHAPTER 2

Three Really Bad Habits

"Self-motivation rather than external motivation is at the heart of creativity, responsibility, healthy behavior, and lasting change. External cunning or pressure can sometimes bring about compliance, but with compliance comes various negative consequences, including the urge to defy."

Edward Deci

Because teachers in private or public schools are not destroying children's love of learning on purpose, it is important to understand what habits they inherited that are causing the problem. There are certainly more than the three we discuss here, but these are crucial:

1. They use data for harm instead of joy. The most common way is ranking. Even in home school, we need a method to avoid the tendency to rank and compare one child to another. The best way to avoid this is to add the contribution of each child together to create a total for the whole family. You will learn how we track individual progress, then how we track "team family" progress.

2. They measure short-term memory instead of what the children really know. The process of cram and forget is nonsense. It starts early with learning spelling words and reading sight words. The children learn the prescribed spelling for the week, take an exam, then forget. You will learn in *How to Create a Perfect Home School* how to always

measure long-term memory. That is what the children really know, not what adults thought they learned.

3. They bribe students to learn. Bribery takes away all the joy. If you learn ___, then I will let you _____.

When children have to be bribed to learn, something is terribly wrong. Learning is as natural as breathing, and we do not know of any teachers who bribe children to breathe. Bribery to learn must become history!

My children are so excited to work as a team (and individually) to get their best scores yet. They cheer each other on, and absolutely no bribery is needed! They are excited to celebrate by creating memories instead of throwaway treasures. We work to earn experiences. We use the game Kerplunk to celebrate each all-time best score. Each of my boys chooses a number located on the base of the game. They make sure that when they get an ATB (all-time best), they move the opening to their number and pull out a stick. That way the marbles fall into their numbered spot. The amount of marbles is in no way associated with how many ATBs they have. Once all the marbles have fallen out of the top, whoever has the most marbles in their numbered spot gets to choose what dessert we eat before dinner that night. It's incredible how exciting this is for them and how easy it is for me. No more bribes in our house! It has completely replaced any need to buy junk to get my children to learn.

You might take note of other habits you inherited that contribute to children's loss of desire to learn. As you realize these habits, it is essential to find replacements for them. *How to Create a Perfect Home School* is full of ways to avoid the three bad habits above.

In my research, I did not ask what percentage of students love learning at school. I only asked what percentage of students love school. I did not ask whether they love school for learning, sports, music, friends, drama, or other reasons. Since the initial research, I have followed up with questions about the love of learning for high school students. The answers show that consistently below 10% of students love learning in high school. The problem is simple to understand. When children lose their will to work hard and gain no thrill from the learning, they do not care about the skill adults believe they should have.

In the next chapter, you will learn how to measure children's will and thrill from year to year. Then in Chapter 4, we will teach the process for measuring skill. The chapters on measuring skill, will, and thrill provide an essential foundation to implement the exciting instructional ideas that follow. Detailed information on skill, will, and thrill is located in Chapter 4 of John Hattie and Kyle Hattie's newest book, *10 Steps to Develop Great Learners: Visible Learning for Parents*.

The structure of *How to Create a Perfect Home School* is approximately one-fourth measurement of learning and three-fourths instructional strategies. *How to Create a Perfect School* has the opposite structure, with much more focus on measurement and one-fourth on instruction. The reason *How to Create a Perfect School* has so little focus on instruction is that it pertains to all teachers, all subjects, and all grade levels. Home educators have no prescribed curriculum to implement. Therefore, *How to Create a Perfect Home School* must provide the knowledge and subsequent confidence for parent educators to avoid giving over control of what, when, and how their children learn to some program author they have never met. Author John Maxwell contrasts leaders who demand with leaders who develop. The teachers are the leaders of the learning and sincerely want to develop the children's skill, will, and thrill. When the skill of a purchased program becomes more important than the children themselves, we say the teacher has become a demanding victim of a program trap.

CHAPTER 3

Measuring the Will and Thrill

"Our schools must preserve and nurture the yearning for learning that everyone is born with. Joy in learning comes not so much from what is learned, but from the learning."

W. Edwards Deming

The two main components of intrinsic motivation are the willingness to work hard and the thrill that comes from learning. The best way to measure children's intrinsic motivation is by asking them about their effort and joy. Their answers are recorded on a practical tool called the Will and Thrill Matrix (Appendix A). Maintaining intrinsic motivation is the most important element in education. Why? Because when students have the desire to work hard and receive great joy from their education, the learning keeps on going and going. There is no ceiling to limit the children's learning.

The advice teachers are given to motivate students to learn is wrong and backward. We want children to pressure the teacher to teach more instead of the teacher pressuring the children to learn more. When educators maintain the natural love of learning, this is exactly what happens—the source of the pressure is reversed.

In *How to Create a Perfect School*, the process for measuring intrinsic motivation for a classroom of students is to collect one dot on the matrix from each student in the classroom. The Will and Thrill Matrix provides both teacher and students with an anonymous picture of the intrinsic motivation of the students. For parent educators, the document becomes a record of intrinsic motivation year after year, much like saving school photos year after year. The overall assessment from all the learning experiences is recorded with a grade level or an age inside the Will and Thrill Matrix. Figure 3.1 shows the first three entries for one student.

Figure 3.1

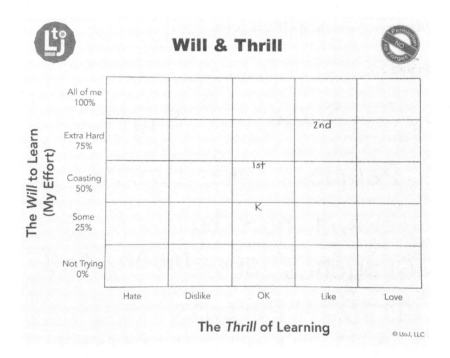

When the dot is not in the upper right corner, ask children what could be done to improve either the thrill or the will. Take the children's advice, when possible, and state, "We will experiment with your idea for the next two weeks, then check to see whether it helped our will or helped our thrill. If it did, we will continue it. If we find out that your hypothesis did not work, we'll brainstorm for other ideas to test out. Appendix B is a sample feedback form for collecting will and thrill suggestions from students. Many educators use the word "feedback" to refer to advice they are giving to students. My preference is to use the word "feedback" as the advice the students are giving the teacher just like any employee can give advice to the boss regarding the improvement of the organization. Vic Cottrell interviewed thousands of teachers during his career studying exemplary teachers and helping school leaders hire exemplary teachers. In his research, he found that only 2% of teachers regularly practice asking students for their assistance to improve the learning in the classroom. When home educators ask for feedback, they shouldn't be surprised if they receive something like this poem.

Figure 3.2

Sweet   Stuff

People   are sweet

and nice but

Grouches are mean and

dirty.   Parents

Are   Half 'n' HALf !

CHAPTER 4

Measuring Skill for Individual Students

"By applying yourself to the task of becoming a little better each and every day over a period of time, you will become a lot better."

John Wooden

The standard way of measuring children's learning is chapter tests. The content for students to learn over a year is divided into chapters in a book, and students take a quiz at the end of each chapter, usually once a week. The process makes perfect sense until one realizes the unintended consequence. Students figure out they need to know the content only for the Friday quiz, then they promptly forget what they studied. The teachers do not say, "It's OK to forget what we did all week." They really want the students to remember. But the system works against the desire of the teachers.

Most of my friends remember that we would memorize for a test, then immediately forget. I vividly remember how challenging I thought math was. I could hardly sit still in my seat before a test because I just wanted the papers to be passed out so that I could write down the formulas I needed to remember. The math did not come easily to me, and I definitely didn't understand "why" I was doing any of the work I was doing. Teachers drilled the "rules" and "cheats" for math into my head, but the actual understanding? It wasn't there. Graduating from college was such a celebration for so many reasons, but a big one was that I was no longer going to be tested on math. As a public-school teacher, I began to appreciate math more, especially when I could help students who were struggling. I saw myself in them. Now that I am educating my own children, I have a deep desire to make sure they fully understand math and don't feel like they need to just memorize the formulas or the cheats. I love finding ways to enjoy and have fun in math, incorporating things the children love. It is such a gift.

Often home educators come together to learn and share stories. I suggest that at one of these events, people share cram-and-forget stories. It will help everyone remember that this is not really education if students only need to remember for the test. I have a college friend who never studied the night before a test because he knew he couldn't remember the content that long. So, on the morning of the test, he set his alarm for 4:00 a.m. to study. He knew he could then remember for the test, and all the content would be gone by noon. Have fun sharing your stories.

Figure 4.1

This logo was created to remind students that the aim is to learn and not to take a quiz and promptly forget.

The process to measure only long-term memory starts at the same place as chapter tests— "What are students to know for the year?" The content can be divided into chapters for instruction, but not for assessment. The key concepts for the year are written down in numerical order. Often this order is the sequence in which the content will be taught.

Sample key concepts for grade 3 math are included in Appendix C. These lists provide both excellent resources for home educators to use and a sample of what is needed to guide learning. Math quizzes that match the key concept lists are available for purchase.

I cannot say enough about these key concept lists and quizzes. These are what I always wanted but never realized I needed. The curriculum I used in prior years went over these concepts, but I felt like the program was in control, not me. These lists guide our school more than almost anything else. Each quiz question is labeled with the key concept it matches, so we can keep track of what concepts my children are getting correct and incorrect. We use a highlighter to mark the concept once the children get it correct. We make tally marks next to the concept each subsequent time it is answered correctly. After about eight or so quizzes, I realized my second grader had gotten questions on measurement correct more than any other concept. It informed my teaching because I knew I needed to focus more on concepts he had yet to get correct. I felt more aware of his strengths and weaknesses than I had ever been with our previous curriculum. Additionally, every week my children get mini lessons on multiple concepts, and I use them as a springboard to introduce a new topic. This has always worked for us because they naturally want to get those questions correct on their next quiz, so they are invested in finding out how to solve the problems.

John Hattie teaches the sequence of learning from surface learning to deep learning and onto transfer learning.

Even though the triangle communicates a sequence, Hattie wants us to understand that the sequence

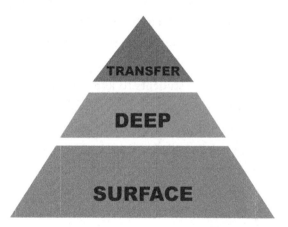

Figure 4.2

is not always present. Surface learning is the foundation. Students often learn literary terms (surface learning) such as idiomatic phrases, similes, and adverbs. After the teacher has taught the definitions and shown students examples from literature, the deep writing assignment would be to utilize one or more of the literary terms in the next writing assignment. Surface is the foundation for the deep. We must all remember that as important as the foundation is in building a house, we do not stop with the foundation; we build upon it. Transfer learning occurs when students see examples of either deep or surface learning in other school subjects or outside of school.

This is why I love Codi Hrouda and Emma McInerney's book How to Create Language Experts with Literary Terms. *My children write all the time about their math work and science work. They also write creative stories. However, their writing doesn't always include the specific literary terms. My kindergartner loves making his own books. His favorite was his book of rhyming words. He included his name in every sentence he wrote along with the rhyming words. He loved reading this every day!*

Our assessment process should always focus upon long-term memory versus short-term memory assessed by chapter tests. The first step for this is to write down all the surface-learning key concepts for the whole year. Utilizing content found on the internet or in curriculums for sale, the home educator creates the list of concepts. One of the most important aspects of this process is not placing trivia on the list. Only what is essential for students to know goes on the list. Trivia is often taught because it is interesting, but trivia should not be on the key concept list.

The hard part about trivia versus essential knowledge is that there are no rules to distinguish between them. It is a matter of the adult's opinion.

Once this list is prepared and handed out to the children, students take a nongraded quiz on a random sample of the whole year's content. The official name of this process is LtoJ®.

The synonym for LtoJ® is review/preview because children are always asked questions about content not yet taught (preview) and content already taught (review). The term LtoJ® comes from the histograms as the shape moves from an L to a bell curve and onto a J curve at year's end. Appendices D, E, and F display the movement for a classroom of students all studying the same content. I include these graphs, so readers know the reasoning behind the label LtoJ®. Rarely are these graphs used in home education because students are not all learning the same content at the same time. However, when groups of home-school students convene, they may want to observe the exciting movement from the L to the bell to the J over the course of a school year.

The notion that adults would ask questions about content not yet taught seems crazy. However, this process has been implemented over 20 years in multiple states. The evidence shows that students love being assessed by answering the question "Did you do better than ever before?" versus "Why didn't you have 100% on the quiz about what I taught you Monday to Thursday this week?"

This was a work in progress with my second grader. He wanted to get every answer correct. It was a constant conversation with him about why we take these quizzes, which I welcome because it opens the lines of communication and presents many other life-experience lessons. With time, he realized that he's trying to beat himself, not get a perfect score each week. Ultimately, he is now pumped up whenever he beats his prior best score. That is his favorite part of school! Can you believe it? A quiz is a child's favorite part of school. Dr. Jenkins told me this would happen, but I had my doubts until I experienced it with my own children.

One day when my second grader's attitude wasn't very good, I sat down with him. I told him we have no choice but to do school. I asked him what our week should look like and what would motivate him. First, he asked for more breaks on the days we spend the most time at our school table. Second, he suggested we do our LtoJ® quizzes on Friday. That way, he has something to look forward to and can choose what math concept he wants to work on the next week. I love this because he feels like he is in control, and we are still getting done what we need to.

The number of questions asked each week is the approximate square root of the number of key concepts for the year. For example, if students need to learn 40 key concepts for the year, select six concepts at random from the 40 for each quiz. If students need to learn 60 key concepts, then select eight at random for each quiz. Some subjects have so much content that the list of key concepts could be 100 or 150 long. Quizzes could be 10 or 12 questions each time. Figure 4.3 is a bucket of 150 spelling words for grade 1. For each of the 28 spelling quizzes, the home educator pulls out 12 words at random. The 12 words are put back into the bucket for the next quiz, when 12 are pulled out at random again. Figure 4.4 is a sample student run chart from first-grade spelling. Remember, the goal is that by the end of the year, the children can spell any 12 words pulled out of the bucket with no studying. The children have placed the spelling of all 150 words into their long-term memory.

Figure 4.3

A sample student run chart for 12 questions is in Appendix G. A complete supply of student run charts is located at LtoJ.net under "Free Resources." Select the graphs for the number of questions for each quiz. All the graphs are created for 28 quizzes during a year. That's seven quizzes per quarter. There is no cost to download blank graphs.

On the student run chart, students are to designate each time they score better than ever before. This is called ATB for "all-time best." There is no ATB for quiz 1; it is merely baseline data. When a student answers every question correctly multiple times, these are also ATBs because outperforming perfect is impossible. Note that on Figure 4.4, Emma did better than ever before eight times; this is designated by "No Permission to Forget" stickers.

Actually, the process is simple, but because it is so unusual it can seem complicated. In review, the process is:

Figure 4.4

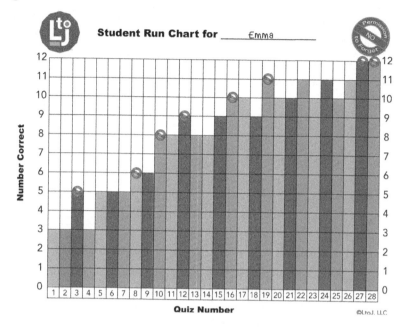

1. Tell the students what they will learn for the year.

2. Quiz the students 28 times a year on questions chosen at random from the key concept list.

3. Have the student graph the number correct after each quiz on a downloaded student run chart.

There are three major reasons for this assessment process:

1. Home educators can assess what is in students' long-term memory because the items are drawn at random.

2. Much of the thrill from learning comes from the visual evidence that the graph is going up and up and up.

3. The data becomes a joyful experience instead of something to be dreaded. No grade or percentage is written on these assessments; the aim is simple—do better than ever before.

As stated earlier, having joyful data of skill attainment is a major way that the will and thrill are maintained at a very high level. You may find that despite all the exciting instructional ideas that follow in *How to Create a Perfect Home School*, these quizzes are often the children's favorite part of the week.

CHAPTER 5

Measuring Skill for Team Family

*"It is not a few star performers who make up a strong team.
It is a collection of many players with good capability
working in unison that makes an exceptional team."*

Jeffrey Liker

As soon as data for each student is placed on a classroom wall, data becomes an instrument for harm instead of a tool for great joy. We explained the progress of individual students in Chapter 4. Put student run charts and the key concept list in a student folder. The key concept list may include Dolch sight words to read, spelling words, math concepts, or Bible events to understand. (The Dolch sight words have been used for many years as a basic list of words children should read instantly. They are readily available on the internet.) Use the content from each key concept list for an LtoJ® quiz 28 times during a school year. Record the results for each student.

Then, add this data from all the quizzes and all family members to display it in family graphs. How are we all doing together? If only one student is in the home school, there are multiple quizzes from multiple key concept lists. Use these separate totals to complete the family run chart.

The family run chart is like a scoreboard at an athletic event, except there is no competing team. The competition is to outperform prior scores. The family run chart is simple addition. How many questions did our family answer correctly? When the family has more correct than ever before, designate it as an ATB for all-time best. The designation can be a written ATB above the highest-ever columns, any small sticker, or the LtoJ® stickers that you can purchase from Amazon with all the books by Lyle Lee Jenkins.

Family run charts are all the same except the possible number of correct answers varies. With one child taking three quizzes of ten questions each, the most possible correct answers is 30. Thus, the family run chart to use is the one with a y-axis of 30. When home schools utilize the math fluency quizzes located at Amazon under Lyle Lee Jenkins, the total questions can be up to 40 on each quiz. Thus, some family run charts have 200 questions as the y-axis.

The family run chart collection download has graphs that reach up to 20, 30, 40, 50, 60, 80, 100, 120, 150, and 200. Home educators select the one closest to what is possible in a perfect week. Located at LtoJ.net under "Free Resources" is a tab for family run charts. These blank family run charts are free to download.

I have two children taking quizzes this year. My second grader has five quizzes. The quizzes have 30, 20, 10, 7, and 10 questions. All four of my kindergartner's quizzes have 10 questions. Altogether, that is 117. We chose the graph that has 120 because that is the closest available.

Remember, the celebrations for *How to Create a Perfect Home School* are for individual ATBs and family ATBs. Parents want their children to cooperate and help each other, and the family run chart is one way to do this.

The family run chart below is from a home-school family with two children. They each took four quizzes a total of 28 times. The total number of correct questions was added together for the eight quizzes each time to create the chart you see. The logo is above each ATB, making it easier to count up the ATBs. The total is 14 out of the 28 weeks.

Figure 5.1

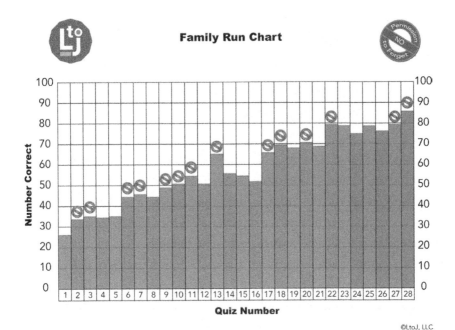

Figure 5.2 is the LtoJ Graphic Review.

Figure 5.2

It summarizes the content of chapters 4 and 5 in one graphic:

1. What are we going to learn this year?
2. We will prove along the way that we are getting closer to knowing the year's content.
3. We are all engaged in creating the graphs.
4. We all celebrate ATBs.

John Hattie researched 250 influences upon student learning using the statistical tool effect sizes. The average effect size from all 250 influences was 0.40. The influence with the largest effect size is collective teacher efficacy with an effect size of 1.57. Thus, the evidence indicates that collective efficacy is four times more effective than the average influence upon student learning. Figure 5.2 and the four steps above provide a clear visual explanation of collective efficacy. In the next chapter, you will learn the effect size of tangible rewards. Remember, this is one of the three bad habits educators inherited that are mentioned in Chapter 2.

Figure 5.3 Collective Teacher Efficacy

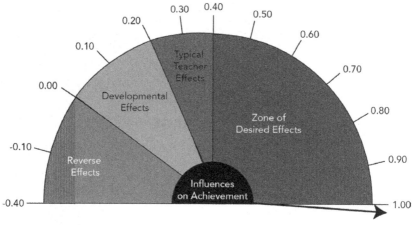

Figure 5.3 is a simple visual that John Hattie used to display all of his research.

Since 0.40 is an average effect size, it is obvious that 125 influences upon learning do not create a year's learning in a year's time whereas there are 125 influences that do create a year's learning in a year's time or even more. Collective teacher efficacy provides almost four times the learning over the average influence. It is 1.57.

CHAPTER 6

What Program Are You Using?

"Reading achievement will not advance significantly until schools act on the fact that it depends on the possession of a broad but definable range of diverse knowledge."

E.D. Hirsch

When home educators convene, a common question is, "What program are you using?" The answer should be, "I do not use a program and here is why."

It is certainly wise to study the table of contents for a program to give you a head start when you create the list of new knowledge for the school year. Some aspects of a program might work quite well during the school year. The point here is for home educators to not give up the decision making to the authors of a program. For home educators, there is a constant search for better ways to teach any item on the annual learning list.

This was hard for me at first! Being a former classroom teacher, I loved the clear beginning and end that I had with curriculum. What I didn't realize is that I had little grasp of all the subject matter that was being taught. I felt the only control I had was to make my kids finish the given lessons (even if they didn't like them). Now that I've let it go, I have a much better idea of what my kids know and how to help them move forward in learning, not just finishing the last assignment. Programs have no way to connect what my children already know to what the programs want children to learn. It is my job to be the connector every day.

I cannot tell you how many public-school teachers wish leaders would just tell them what children need to know by the end of the year. Then, let the teachers use their creativity to teach, and let them prove at the end of the year the children learned the content. Since home educators are free from mandated programs, it is imperative they do not fall into the same failed program trap.

With programs, when a child doesn't understand a concept, the temptation is to bribe the child to complete the program directive. Bribing for learning is an admission of failure. Even worse, the evidence (Hattie and Hattie, *Visible Learning for Parents*, p. 63) shows that rewarding students makes learning worse. Figure 6.1 shows the same barometer figure as in Chapter 5 but with the research from tangible rewards. The effect size from these tangible rewards is a negative; not even a smidgen of learning growth. Collective efficacy creates four times the learning, and all the money on tangible rewards makes learning worse!

Roadblocks to learning create a detective mind-set in the home educator to learn how others have successfully taught the content. With a program, adults feel compelled to follow it page by page or activity by activity. Children do not need to learn page by page. This systematic approach removes the creative teaching style children need to maintain intrinsic motivation.

Figure 6.1

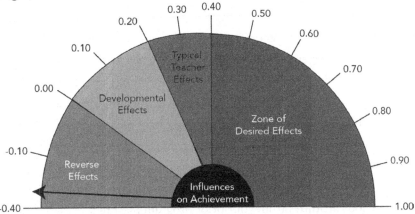

Ask yourself or friends to describe their journey to learn something about which they are quite knowledgeable. Their journey is not a step-by-step process. It is almost always a random learning journey. After expertise is developed, the brain organizes all these random learnings into a nice, logical sequence. When a roadblock occurs with children learning a particular concept, set it aside until a later time. There is no sequence more important than children understanding what is taught. Look around for answers regarding how to teach the content. Look for strategies that will connect with children's prior knowledge and make sense to them.

This was a very difficult concept for me to grasp. I was trying to essentially shove the alphabet down my 4-year-old's throat. I would sit there with flash cards or even a fun game and practice. He hated it. He just refused to learn the alphabet. "Why does he need to know it now?" Dr. Jenkins asked. I was flabbergasted, because of course he needs to know it now! Very hesitantly, I trusted his guidance, took a step back, and lo and behold, my 4-year-old turned into a 5-year-old who knew his alphabet. I learned that I had become accustomed to the idea that knowing the alphabet has to come first. The beauty of home school is that the sequence and design is yours to create and can change with each child.

No, you do not have a program. What you have is much more structured than any program on the market. You *know* what your children will learn for the complete year. You know if they are on target to learn all the content by year's end, and along the way you are assured that intrinsic motivation is being protected. Programs are things, not people. Thus, the program doesn't care if the children love learning. For teachers who have children for only a year, the program may be considered a success even if children hate learning. However, since you are the teacher again next school year and the following year, children need both the content to be learned and intrinsic motivation maintained. You do not need to inherit sour attitudes from your prior program teaching.

We understand that building enough confidence in home educators so that making program purchases unnecessary is a huge challenge. Therefore, we wrote *How to Create a Perfect Home School*.

Think of your home-school journey as a metaphor for the navigator guiding a ship across the ocean. The navigator, at a minimum, needs a compass and precise latitude and longitude.

The compass for the home-school teacher journey is the key concept list. What are we going to learn this year? Do not confuse a key concept list with a syllabus. A syllabus is what the professor is going to teach this year, and it may not have much to do with what the students learn or even what is on the final exam.

The latitude is the grade level or the age. Simple.

The longitude is the learning location from the LtoJ® quizzes. After 25% of the school year is over, does the child know 25% of the content as evidenced by quiz results? After 60% of the year has passed, does the child know 60% of the annual content? Where are we at each step of the way on this yearlong learning journey? Appendix H is a sample grade 3 math standards quiz with questions matching the key concept list in Appendix C. Appendix I is a sample math fluency quiz for third grade. Think of math standards as the destination for the car and math fluency as the car to take us there in the least time. Standards are the content to be learned, and the wheels enable students to get to the destination much faster.

The compass was discovered in the 1300s. The latitude was known for centuries if the stars, moon, or sun were visible. A way to know longitude in the middle of the ocean was not widely accepted until 1767. Education still does not have a way for parents to ascertain the longitude for their children's learning. Yes, we have ABCDF grades, which are like measuring how many fathoms deep the water is at the present time, but we don't really have a way of measuring the understanding needed to fully grasp a concept.

Knowing the target has made school so much easier for me and my children. We don't finish the school year when the book is done. We finish the school year because we have arrived at the destination.

CHAPTER 7

Starting Reading and Writing Perfectly

"Praising children's intelligence harms their motivation,
and it harms their performance."

Carol Dweck

Perfect

Perfect is maintaining the desire to learn that is inborn in every child. The evidence that this desire is being maintained is that the children still have the tenacity to work to learn and receive joy from learning. The challenge for all teachers is keeping this inborn love of learning alive while at the same time helping the child gain the knowledge appropriate for their age. We wrote the contents of this chapter to guide parents as they naturally prepare children for future competency in reading and writing.

My kindergartner can be very resistant to learning when it's not his idea. He has in his mind what he wants school to be, and most of the time it is drastically different from how I want it to be. Therefore, we have had to be very creative with school during his kindergarten year. There is a lot less pushing and a lot more listening and gently guiding on my part. This being said, getting him to write has been challenging. However, if he is allowed to create some sort of art, he is more than willing to dictate a story to me. Sometimes he will dictate more than 10 sentences. He has a vivid and incredibly creative imagination. He creates his own characters on a regular basis, so telling their stories is exciting for him. Afterward, I will encourage him to trace over my words. Depending on how much he dictated, it could be a few words or a few sentences. Almost never will I have him trace over all the words because it is too overwhelming for him.

Reading and Writing Foundation

Learning to read and write is more a function of the ears than the eyes. It is impossible for parents to deposit too many stories, poems, books, nursery rhymes, and songs into their children's brains. Then there are thousands of conversations explaining how something works, utilizing and explaining with precise language. Oral language serves as the foundation for becoming a successful reader and writer.

For example, from all this listening, children learn that "I Grandma's yesterday house went to" doesn't sound right. Likewise, they know "I went to Grandma's house yesterday" sounds correct. Later when learning to read, children know that a word that starts with "ho" is probably house or home, based upon the context of the story. When children with a huge vocabulary are learning to read, they can almost always figure out an unknown word with the context of the sentence and the phonics of the first one or two letters. It is the deposit of thousands of oral experiences that provides such ease with unknown words.

Step 1

Beyond listening to oral language, the formal reading and writing process begins with dictation. Parents write down what their children say. This can begin at a very early age. The purpose is for children to learn that words on paper are the same words people speak. As parents write their children's statements, they speak out loud about spelling, capital letters, and syllables. The parents save this collection of dictated sentences and stories as material to read back to children. Young children learn that reading and writing use the same sentences and words they speak.

My 3-year-old daughter tends to sit at the school table and draw during school. She already has dictated such fun stories about her pictures. It is so fun to hear what is in her mind at such a young age!

Adding Flavor

Some of parents' most enjoyable dictation times will be recording what their children say about art they created. The art comes first. It is followed by dictation. The art can be a "realistic" creation that the child can explain, or it can be purely lines and shapes as children explain what they see in the abstraction. Below are two examples from a classroom. The first is a scribble. The second is paint squirted on one-half of a sheet of art paper, with the paper then folded and mirror symmetry created on the other side of the page.

Figure 7.1

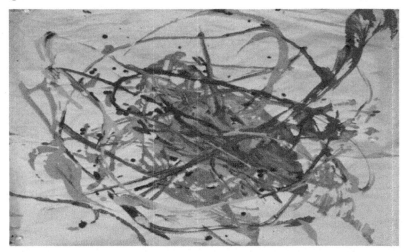

This is a rainbow that didn't know how to make a bend.
by drew

Figure 7.2

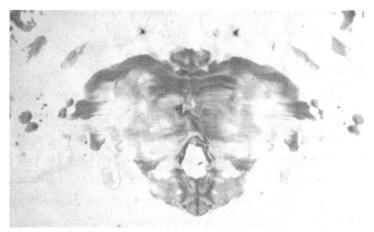

My buTTerfly goes To the flower To Talk To The flower.

The progression for dictation is:

1. The adult takes dictation, writing in pen.

2. The adult writes some letters or words in pencil, with the remainder in pen. The child traces over the adult pencil writing.

3. Finally, the adult writes the whole story in pencil, and the child traces over the story in pen.

The two previous pictures are at the next level of progression; there was no dictation. The children wrote in pencil, had the stories edited by an adult, then traced over the edited writing.

Summary

The two aspects of the reading and writing foundation are:

1. Pour language into the child's mind from printed sources and conversations.

2. Retrieve language from the child through dictation.

The two steps are greatly influenced by children's interests. Follow them.

Back to Perfect

In the hustle of life among young children, it is far too easy to make a video the center of development instead of books, dictation, and conversations. Remember that all the time invested in the foundational activities will pay great dividends when children are learning to read and write for themselves. The inborn desire to learn is much easier to maintain with a solid foundation.

One way for parents to ascertain how reading progress is moving along is to use the Dichotomous Reading Rubric. As children read, listen and determine where they are improving over time. The rubric is not for evaluating children, but it is for feedback to the home educator who is wondering how well the child is reading. The typical grade-level expectation for grade 1 students is 50–60 words per minute, grade 2 is

Figure 7.3

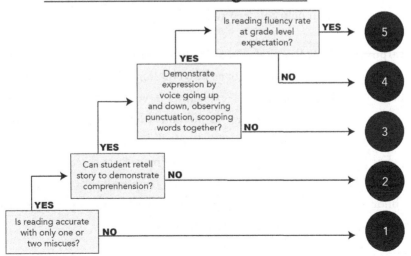

Dichotomous Reading Rubric

100–120 words per minute, and grade 3 is 150 words per minute or higher. See Figure 7.3 for the Dichotomous Reading Rubric. This is also Appendix J.

You want your children to learn how to read well. After that, you want your children to desire to read. Both desires can be accomplished over time. The responsibilities listed below will guide you on this joyful journey.

Do not think of learning to read as knowledge to be inserted into a child's head such as historical events, definitions, mathematics formulas, and so on. Reading is more like learning how to swim. Any swimming coach can write down a dozen or more skills that swimmers have. However, coaches know they cannot print out the list, teach the items one at a time, check the items off as learned, and throw the student into the deep end of the pool. Reading is the same. Learning how to read is not a checklist as much as we would like it to be. "Learn the names of the letters, learn the sounds of the letters, learn about diphthongs and blends, and then you'll be a reader" is an incomplete strategy. If reading was a list of skills that once learned would guarantee reading success, there would not be so many children struggling with reading in the United States. The skills are taught and re-taught and taught again. Reading is not simple, yet home educators can learn how to help children read just like the coach can help children swim.

Responsibility 1: Remember that learning to read has more to do with ears than with eyes. Pour language into children constantly. Accomplish this by reading, singing, and explaining everyday items and events with as much detailed language as possible. How many words could a truck-driver parent teach to a child about all the components of a truck?

For home educators, I recommend reading at least three times a day to children. Vary between picture books, chapter books, and poetry. Children are never too old to listen and view the art of great picture books and never too young for chapter books.

Responsibility 2: Do not stop connecting oral and written language. This is primarily accomplished by adults taking dictation from the child and pointing out some details of the language during the writing. Dictation is often about art. Children know that when they complete the art, they will dictate sentences about the art and later write on their own.

Art ideas abound, but here are a few:

+ The child can create free-form art with watercolors, paints, or colored pencils. The child can create art with Pattern Blocks and reproduce with the Pattern Block Template.

+ The teacher and child can use Ed Emberley's *Thumbprint* and *Fingerprint* books for unlimited art ideas

+ The teacher can find a tangram puzzle that interests the child, and the child can solve and reproduce with a tangram template.

+ The child can fold a piece of paper in half, squirt paint on it, and smash it together. The teacher can then write what the child sees.

+ A successful technique for children's art is studying the art of a favorite children's book illustrator and copying the style.

Responsibility 3: Help the child write for themselves. Have the children write with a pencil. When they are done, the adult can erase and correct errors. Then the child traces over the edited writing with a felt pen. During the tracing process, children will make errors. Educators can use white Avery dots to cover the errors and allow the child to keep working. We must always remember that reading and writing live next door to each other, and they should be the best of neighbors. The dictation described in Responsibility 2 does not disappear here. It is very common for young children's hands to get tired before the story in their head is complete. They will write "The End" when they are nowhere near the end of the story. The adult can pick up the pencil and take dictation to complete the story.

The tracing-over process could start with only a few words left for the child to trace over. The teacher could also do something else, like leave all letter T's available for the child to trace. For young children, I suggest giving them paper that will not tear when they erase and that has the widest line spaces you can find. I would not use lined paper that has dotted lines between the solid lines except when you teach letter formation. The dotted lines slow down the children's flow of creative thoughts.

Responsibility 4: Point out simple phonics patterns that naturally appear while carrying out the prior responsibilities. The adults need to know that no letter in English is pronounced the same way 100% of the time. However, there are phonics generalizations—patterns that normally you can depend upon. It is easy to overwhelm children with too many of these generalizations, so be careful. Rhyming words are interesting to children. Similar spelling patterns are fun: yet, pet, jet, and wet all seem to work out quite well, and then along comes debt. The book *Who's Afraid of a Lion: Aesop's Bully Fable* has the bully gnat taunting the lion with blends. Once the children can read the book, it is time to look for other blend examples.

Responsibility 5: Build a collection of words the child wants to read. This keeps alive the belief "I can read" along this journey of responsibilities. In a study done years ago with the words chosen by 180 first-grade children, each with 50–80 words, almost half the words were science words. They asked for four times more science words than fantasy words.

Figure 7.4

My kindergartner's word book consisted of places he loves to visit (mountains, Disneyland, etc.), our pets' names, and types of animals. He loved drawing the pictures and practicing the big words each day!

The "caveman" important word is from the first week in kindergarten. The teacher asked the child what word he wanted to learn to read, and she wrote it on a flash card and then in the "important word book." The student wrote "caveman" five times on a small whiteboard, drew a picture, and wrote "caveman" below the teacher's writing.

Figure 7.5

Responsibility 6: Build a collection of books and dictated stories the child can read. Children must never get into the habit of "barking at the print," which is sounding out words in a very painful, slow way. They must hear themselves read at a normal pace. Adults should experiment with speaking to a child at 20–25 words per minute. It is very difficult to understand speech spoken so slowly. Likewise, it is very hard to comprehend reading unless it is being read at least 50–60 words per minute. The child can read easy readers and dictated stories at almost the speed an adult would read them.

Responsibility 7: Have the child finish learning all the letter names and know how to write each of the 52 lower- and upper-case letters. By now, children know all or almost all the letters. Complete the learning so children know them all. The reason for knowing letter names is not for reading; it is for spelling and communication with others. Children do not need to know the letter names to learn how to read, but they do need to know the letter names for communication. For example, imagine this conversation:

Adult: What is your name?
Child: Knox.
Adult: Do you spell it N-O-X?
Child: No. It is spelled K-N-O-X.

Adult: What is your name?
Child: Silas.
Adult: Do you spell it S-I-G-H-L-A-S?
Child: No, it is spelled S-I-L-A-S.

Adult: What is your name?
Child: Amelie.
Adult: Do you spell it A-M-I-L-E-E?
Child: No, it is spelled A-M-E-L-I-E.

Learning how to read should be so painless that children forget how they learned to read. Human beings are very good at taking any process and making it more complicated. The process of learning how to read is certainly no exception. Let's keep reading joyful, simple, and fun.

CHAPTER 8

Nitty Gritty Language: Sight Words, Spelling, Editing, and Literary Terms

"In a poll of 143 creativity researchers, there was wide agreement about the number one ingredient in creative achievement— perseverance and resilience."

Carol Dweck

These four topics form the basics of what society expects from educated students. Children should recognize certain words immediately without trying to sound them out. They are called sight words and most often the Dolch Sight Words. With spell checker and other advances in word processing, spelling success is much easier than before. Nevertheless, society does expect educated people to be able to spell common words without a computer. The two extremes regarding editing are both wrong. They are the red pen and inventive spelling. Inventive spelling just means leave spelling alone; enjoy the child's creativity. Both the red pen and inventive spelling should be replaced by the eraser and editing. From words like "adjective" to "simile," society has agreed upon definitions of ways to communicate with language. Spelling is clearly a part of these agreements. Elementary school is where children learn these basics for future communication success.

Dolch Sight Words

Sight words are called "sight" because children are expected to read them instantly, and they are not phonetic. One example is the word "right," which phonetically would be spelled "rite" or "write." Giving children practice and confidence with these words that appear in almost every story makes sense.

There is a simple way to measure progress with Dolch Sight Words, which are the most well-known words children should know instantly. Select a portion of them, put them in a bucket, draw the designated number of words out of the bucket, place them on a table in front of the child, and merely state, "Find the words you can read and read them to me." The number of words read correctly is graphed on the student run chart described in Chapter 4.

50   words — Select 8 each quiz and download student run chart for 8 questions.

100 words — Add 50 more to the bucket that has the original 50 words. Quiz the student on 10 words.

150 words — Add 50 more to the bucket of 100 prior words. Quiz the student on 12 words.

200 words — Add the last 50 or more to the bucket of words. Quiz the student on 16 words.

The reason for not leaving behind prior words is that children come to think they do not need "those words" anymore. "We are done with them."

How do you know it is time to add more words? It is when the student correctly reads all the randomly selected words seven times in a row. The promotion to the next list is earned and feels great to students. It is called "testing out."

It seems everyone is tempted to put back in the bucket only the words the child missed. Terrible idea! Why? The bucket of words becomes harder and harder to read, and the total number of words read correctly and graphed goes down. A graph that shows on each quiz I know fewer and fewer words is one quick way to destroy intrinsic motivation.

This is worth repeating: Direct the child to find the words they know and read them to you. When Dolch words are flashed to children, they think they are supposed to sound out the words. It cannot be done. These words are called sight words because they are not phonetic. These are words to know instantly the second they are seen.

When I first started homeschooling, the curriculum I used would assess sight words using lists. My second grader would need to read an entire list correctly to move to the next one. Consistently, there was only one or two words he'd miss, then he'd feel defeated because he couldn't move to the next one. It was incredibly discouraging because even though he could read 90% of the words, he was still not "good enough." It was also hard to continue to do any school after he melted down. Soon it became a fight to get him to practice any sight words. That is until I used the LtoJ® method. Once I took the words, cut them up, and assessed him on 10 each week, he began to feel more accomplished because he would count how many he was getting correct instead of how many incorrect. I would say, "Find the words you can read and read them to me." It soon became his favorite LtoJ® quiz because he felt so successful!

Spelling

Two aspects of spelling instruction are (1) learning selected words that occur often in normal life experiences and (2) helping children spell correctly when they ask, "How do you spell_____?"

The sad pattern of cramming and forgetting begins with children studying words on Thursday night, taking the spelling test on Friday, and forgetting how to spell the words on Saturday. The process is the same as described above for Dolch words, except instead of asking children to read words, they are asked to spell words.

Home educators should select the words they desire with other lists used as suggestions. My recommendation is to use approximately 50%

of the words most needed for successful writing, 25% from commonly misspelled lists, 15% from the Bible, and 10% geography. The geography words should be cities, states, rivers, mountains, and lakes that are locally important. Later add national and international words such as Washington, DC, and Australia.

The structure for the word lists and quizzes is below:

Grade	Total	Words per quiz	Number of Words Each Quiz
1	12	150 words	12 randomly selected words
2	16	200 new words	12 grade 2 words; four grade 1
3	20	300 new words	16 grade 3, three grade 2, one grade 1
4	24	400 new words	18 grade 4, four grade 3, two grade 2
5	24	400 new words	18 grade 5, four grade 4, two grade 3
6	24	400 new words	18 grade 6, four grade 5, two grade 4

Here's the biggest change from traditional spelling tests: No longer are children assessed on their short-term memory from what they memorized the night before. The words for the weekly spelling quiz are selected randomly at the time of the quiz. This way home educators know precisely what children know. The idea is that at the end of the school year, every child can spell correctly whatever words are drawn out of the respective grade-level buckets. Do not think that teaching is random; teaching is not random. Only the assessment is random so that long-term memory is assessed. Teaching is logical. Teach the spelling words in any sequence that makes sense for instruction or matches student interest. Gradually over the course of a school year, home educators will know if the instruction stuck in children's long-term memory.

Home educators should be willing to help children spell words anytime during the day. When a child asks an adult how to spell a word, please do not give the child a spelling lesson. When children learn that asking how to spell a word creates an interrupting lesson, they merely stop asking. It is simple: tell the child how to spell the word. Even simpler, the child brings *My Custom Dictionary* to the adult, opened up to the correct page, and the adult writes the word in the spelling dictionary. The child then copies the correct spelling into the work at hand.

My second grader would dread asking for a word to be spelled because I would ask, "How do you think you spell it?" Then he would lose his train of thought because he'd need to practice spelling whatever word he was asking about. I realize this in hindsight. Now, because I don't try to give him a mini spelling lesson each time he asks, he is starting to spell better. This is probably because he's more willing to ask me now!

A master page for creating *My Custom Dictionary* is Appendix K. Duplicate this page 26 times and write letter names for each page. Or you can order a completed dictionary located on Amazon under Lyle Lee Jenkins.

Editing

The red pen is a failed practice. It comes from a general belief in all aspects of life that quality can be inspected into the results. No, quality must be built in all along the way. Building quality along the way is equally important in business and in education. At the other extreme is what has been called inventive spelling. The idea is to ignore correct spelling. People created this idea to avoid the red pen problem, but they solved nothing.

Editing is the correct answer. Students write in pencil and then sit with an adult while they edit the work for spelling, grammar, capitalization, and punctuation. This adult/child time is a powerful learning time as the adult explains along the way the corrections they made. Do not overlook the power of this time. It is easy to think, "Who has time for this?" I learned this from Marion Nordberg with 32 children ages 5–8 who found the time to edit with all her children. Make time for the powerful learning during editing time.

Give the youngest children the opportunity to trace over the edited writing with a felt pen. This gives them practice writing the text correctly. Obviously, children can make a mistake with the felt pen that cannot be erased. Students can place white Avery dots over the error and continue tracing.

The adult writing the word correctly is the quickest way to give children the spelling and let them return to the project that created the spelling need. As the children return to their work, they often give themselves the spelling lesson. They see what they were missing in their attempts. Other times, the children realize that they were phonetically correct, but the word had a silent letter and is spelled differently than one would think. An example from Arizona, where we live, is the cactus word "saguaro," which is pronounced su-whar-o.

I used to either hover and correct my second grader's mistakes as he made them or wait and make him do all the erasing and rewriting. Neither worked, and it makes me cringe that I used to do this. Now he's able to freely write, and we schedule a time (either right then, later that day, or the next day) to go over it so that I can proofread. What I love about this is that I do all the erasing and writing during the proofreading process, and I am able to explain all the corrections. Proofreading this way has allowed conversations around grammar and sentence structure to come more easily. It is the constant communication around language instead of a standalone lesson. My second grader has expressed a desire to learn more about quotation marks and commas because he wants to include them in his writing, so we talk about them frequently. I remember teaching lessons like these in my classroom as a public-school teacher. Everything was taught separately. We would have a lesson and worksheet on quotation marks and a separate lesson and worksheet on commas. What I know now is that the presence of language, reading, writing, and proofreading as a regular part of our schooling routine has allowed for skills to develop in a much deeper, more significant way.

Home educators should use *My Custom Dictionary* year after year until children complete their elementary school education. The children will soon look in their dictionary to see if they have the needed word prior to asking an adult. Sometimes the youngest children do not realize they already have the word in their dictionary. When this occurs, merely circle the word with an eraser, and the eraser crumbs will last long enough for the children to copy the word into their story.

Note the lines are very close together in the spelling dictionary. The reason is that adults write in the dictionary, then the children copy from the dictionary into their work. It is the job of the students to open the dictionary to the correct page when they ask adults to write a word for them. This usually works except when the first letter of a word is silent, or words like "city." Should the word start with a "c" or an "s"?

Literary Terms

Looking over a list of literary terms causes many adults to think their children might be bored learning all of them. These adults are correct. One solution to the problem is to allow children to use their creativity to write about each of the literary terms. Codi Hrouda and Emma McInerney's book *How to Create Language Experts with Literary Terms* has booklet covers, blank pages for student writing, space for student art, and a page of questions about the literary term. The creativity that proceeds from children learning literary terms is wonderful. A third-grade student writing her book of suffixes chose the word "kissing" for one of her words in My Book of Suffixes. She drew a picture of her mom and dad kissing and then wrote, "I love it when my mom and dad are kissing."

The premise of *How to Create a Perfect Home School* is that children can learn all the expected content for their age *and* at the same time maintain their intrinsic motivation. It is much easier to give students boring materials to complete and bribe them to do the work. However, the boredom/bribe sequence is not the reason parents chose to homeschool. Every effort to maintain intrinsic motivation and at the same time become an expert learner is to be applauded.

Codi and Emma's book *How to Create Language Experts with Literary Terms* has at least eight booklets for each grade level K–6. Completing these projects for literary terms in all of elementary school provides a solid foundation with the literary terms students are expected to learn and remember.

What has been most notable to me about these booklets is that although the authors have separated literary terms per grade level, the terms can be learned at the pace of each individual child. For example, when my sons were 7 and 5, they absolutely loved learning about homophones. Homophones are in the third-grade set of books, but my boys were ready to learn early. The book became a fun activity for them to do because, to them, it almost felt like a game to find more words that sounded the same but were different. I'm so thankful I had the books available so that I was able to support them right when they were ready to learn. I've also noticed that this is an especially useful tool for my son who has a very creative mind. The fact that he can draw as part of his work allows him to be more invested. He absolutely loves reading the books he writes!

Figure 8.1

My Book of Sentences with Question Marks

Write sentences with question marks

_____

_____

_____

_____

_____

_____

_____

_____

By: _____

Date: _____

School: _____ Teacher: _____

Circle the question mark in each sentence below:

1. What is your cat's name?

2. I like dogs.

3. Who is taller?

4. When is your birthday?

5. We got ice cream!

6. How old are you?

7. I am two years old.

Copy sentences with question marks from your favorite book:

_____

_____

_____

_____

_____

_____

_____

_____

CHAPTER 9

Wisdom from Bill Martin Jr.

"The most important reading skill is for children
to know they can 'make a go' of reading."

Bill Martin Jr.

I began the acknowledgements in *How to Create a Perfect School* with a quotation from Mark Batterson. He wrote, "God is in the business of strategically placing us in the right place at the right time" (Batterson, 2006, p. 12). God arranged for my Bill Martin Jr. friendship, learning, and mentoring. Bill's influence continues to this day. Without him, I would never have known how to write the Bible Patterns for Young Readers or Aesop Patterns for Young Readers series.

After I spent seven years of intense learning about teaching elementary school mathematics in a way that made sense to young minds, a consulting firm hired me to conduct mathematics workshops across the United States and Canada. As a bonus I was able to attend, at no charge, all the workshops conducted by other speakers from the same firm. One of the speakers was Bill Martin Jr. I loved his perspective on reading and children, and at the morning break I introduced myself as a fellow speaker with the same firm. Bill invited me to lunch, and we were friends until his death. I brought him to speak every place where I was employed, then traveled with my wife to many locales accompanying Bill.

Bill was so consistent in his thinking and teaching. As I write this chapter, I can hear his passionate pleas to give children the joy of reading without robbing them of literary joy for life. Below are some of the constant teachings of my friend Bill Martin Jr.

He always wanted teachers to know that children gain reading skill by using their ears to guide their eyes in reading.

He wanted teachers to have multiple ways to help children to unlock print. The belief that "sounding out" was the only strategy for unlocking print irritated him greatly. He also knew that what works for one child doesn't necessarily work for other children. He appreciated how inventive children are and never wanted to discourage their creativity—even in the process of learning to read.

Bill stressed that words have meaning because of the sentence where they are found. Children use their creativity to recognize unknown words to a great extent because of the sentence structure.

Bill loved reading his books to audiences and wanted teachers to have this same joy. *The Ghost-Eye Tree* was one of his favorite books to read aloud. I heard it often. (A recording of *The Ghost-Eye Tree* by Jeff Babcock is available on YouTube.) Use the read aloud time to teach principles of how language is put together by the author. For example, read a book without any punctuation. This helps children understand that punctuation is used by the author to organize words so the story makes sense.

Read the book again, leaving out language for children to finish. With *The Ghost-Eye Tree*, pause as the children fill in what the sister said. Finally, read the book once with an equal pause between each word, then read by chunking the words together in groups. The children will see that authors often chunk words; the most famous chunking is probably "once upon a time." Point out the many chunks as you read aloud to children. Bill loved to make book publishers organize words in chunks, instead of using the whole line of print.

Another common Bill Martin Jr. piece of advice was to give children time to correct themselves. Before jumping in to correct miscues in reading, wait to see if the child thinks, "This is not making sense." The child then goes back over the prior sentence to figure out a way for it to make sense. If the child does not self-correct, the adult can help by reading back exactly how the child read the paragraph. Then the child is given a chance to figure out how to read the text so that it does make sense.

Bill wanted children to enjoy words like "supercalifragilisticexpialidocious." Do not be afraid of big words. Children want to know the difference between a fox and a coyote. They do not want misguided adults to only let them read fox because "coyote" could be a two-syllable word (or a three-syllable word depending on where you live).

Bill wanted educators to always know that word order is so important in unlocking print. Read "oak old tree" instead of "old oak tree" to point out how much they know about word order. (Even my word processor doesn't like "oak old"; it gives me an error message.) Also, look for books to read to children with structures that can be depended upon like ABC; numbers; days of the week; months of years; holidays; seasons; and any other trusted, dependable sequence.

And then, the best Bill Martin Jr. advice: The most important reading skill is for children to know they can "make a go" of reading. The same brain that "made a go" of talking will "make a go" of reading.

I attended a university in Kansas as an undergrad, and Bill Martin Jr. played a big part in my education there. His books were always showcased in my classes because he was a Kansas native. The Bill Martin Jr. Picture Book Award was always a big deal in the elementary schools I worked at and in my college classes. The books that received the award (or were nominated for the award) were showcased on top of bookshelves in the library. We were given lists of these books as well; it was a high honor. Once I graduated, I can say with confidence that I knew more about Bill Martin Jr.'s books and felt more confidence in him as an author than any other children's book author. It is an honor to know that not only did he create great books, but he was an incredible educator who was passionate about getting children to read. It feels only right that my world collided with Dr. Jenkins, who was friends with Bill Martin Jr. These like minds have had a profound impact on my home-school journey.

After reading some of Bill Martin Jr.'s thoughts about reading instruction, one might think Bill was ahead of his time or way off base. Actually, Bill was old school. There are only three approaches to reading. Educators can begin with sounds, words, or sentences. In the middle of the 20th century, students were taught to read with the Dick and Jane series of short books. Dick and Jane utilized the word approach. The authors used a small set of words for the first story, then in each subsequent story added a couple of new words and kept the former words. Before that, almost all reading instruction was with the sentence approach utilizing current literature of the time. The collection of this literature was labeled the McGuffey Readers. Currently, most schools begin with the sound approach, which has been labeled the phonics approach. Over time, the three approaches gain new names, often for marketing purposes. But there are only the three. Clearly, no matter which approach is stressed, there are sounds, words, and sentences. It is a matter of emphasis.

It is very important for all educators to know that none of the three approaches is 100% successful. When a child seems to be making inadequate progress, there are two other options. Utilize whatever works well. If your child loves phonics worksheets keep on going down that path. Remember the aim of *How to Create a Perfect Home School* is for children to maintain the will to work hard and the thrill from the learning while learning the skills.

Many resources for learning to read that utilize the sound or word approaches are available for purchase. However, there are not so many resources utilizing the sentence approach. Therefore, in Appendix L is the Matrix for Sentence Approaches for Reading. It is a 2-by-2 matrix. Each cell describes how to use the combination of art and writing, with children and adults utilizing their talents. Bill Martin Jr.'s books, the Bible Patterns for Young Readers series, and the Aesop Patterns for Young Readers series all fit into the upper right corner of the matrix, with both art and language provided by adults. In the lower left corner of the matrix, the reading material is illustrated and written by children. As stated earlier, this begins with dictation and continues with children

Figure 9.1

writing their own stories. In the upper left corner of the Matrix for Sentence Approaches for Reading is a space for adult art and child language. Wordless books are utilized for this reading activity. *What Will Bear, Rabbit and Chipmunk Do Next?* Figure 9.1 is the cover of Jim Chansler's first wordless book entitled *What Will Bear, Rabbit and Chipmunk Do Next?* The structure is for children to dictate or write the words for the book.

Remember Bill Martin Jr. said that the most important reading skill for children to learn is that they can "make a go" of reading.

The bottom right of the Sentence Approach to Reading Matrix is adult language and child art. Usually, the process is for adults to make a booklet with the words of a song page by page. The children provide the illustrations. When I have observed this, the children illustrate the first page, then realize they cannot read the second page. So, they go back to Page 1 and recite the words to the song they know, then they can read Page 2. This pattern continues on and on. The children cannot read Page 3, so they go back to Page 1 and quickly read the first two pages. Then they know what Page 3 says. Again, we are "making a go" of reading.

One of my favorite reading memories is a book my kindergartner made. He was adamant that he did not want me to teach him how to read. He refused to write, and liked to pretend he didn't even know the alphabet (spoiler alert: he did). Since he loves books, listening to music, and coloring, I printed out a "book" that I made with the words to "Kookaburra Sits in an Old Gum Tree." Each page had a few lines at the very bottom, so he had plenty of room to draw pictures. Once he was finished, he would read the book over and over. There were several nights that he even slept with it!

Figure 9.2 are sample pages and illustrations from the Kookaburra Song Book and a child illustrating the book.

Figure 9.2

CHAPTER 10

Number Sense for a Lifetime

"Encouragement is oxygen for the soul."

John Maxwell

When adults learn the content of this chapter and the How to Create Math Experts series, they always exclaim, "Oh, how I wish I knew this math when I was a child!" Each of the books provides assignment pages for an individual math tool: Pattern Blocks, Base Ten Blocks, tangrams, Geoblocks, Fraction Slices, and math balance. The books move on from the foundation of number sense developed with the content from this chapter.

The foundation for future success with whole numbers, fractions, and measurement is taught with variations of a simple game for three players. There is every reason to begin teaching these various games to children as young as 3.

I taught fourth grade in public school. It was my second year teaching, and my co-teacher (who had been teaching for more than 20 years) reminded me again and again how kids would come into fourth grade with no number sense. She was so frustrated that our district gave us a curriculum map that didn't begin with reviewing place value. "These kids have no idea about place value!" she said. She always spent the first month teaching and re-teaching place value and was adamant that it would make the rest of the year easier. It made me nervous. As a new teacher, I wanted to "follow the rules." I never spent as much time on place value, and it showed. The fourth graders struggled to understand the "why" and "how" all year long in math. How can you understand "carrying" in math if you don't understand where you put the hundreds, tens, and ones? In hindsight, my co-teacher couldn't have been more correct. Number sense is incredibly important. In order to move forward in math, it is vital that students have a good grasp on numbers and place value.

*The Basic Game Is Race for a 100-block.

There are three players. One player is the banker who starts with twenty-five 1-blocks, twenty-five 10-blocks, and one 100-block. Label a blank die with six numerals such as 9, 12, 7, 3, 8, 15. The first player rolls the die. The banker gives the first player the number of blocks they rolled on the die. Then the second player rolls the die and receives the blocks. The two players take turns rolling the die and receiving the blocks. When a player has 10 or more 1-blocks, they trade them for a 10-block. The winner of the game is the first person to trade ten 10-blocks for a 100-block. Very often the game is played three times, with each player having an opportunity to be the banker.

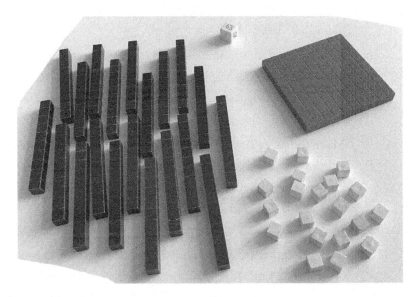

Figure 10.1

Adjusting the Basic Game

This basic game is adjusted continually. Different numerals are written on blank dice, and the name of the game is changed with a slight difference.

1. *Race for 200. Make the numerals on the die larger so that there are approximately ten rolls of the die by each player before there is a winner. Suggested numerals for the die are 15, 25, 30, 12, 21, 20.

2. *Race to Go for Broke. Each player starts with the 100-block and gives back to the banker the number of blocks shown on the die. Suggested numerals for this die are 10, 5, 15, 8, 2, 12.

3. *Roll a pair of dice and add them together. Suggested numerals for this pair of dice are 9, 1, 8, 2, 7, 3. Make both dice the same.

4. *Roll a pair of dice and the player receives the larger number. Suggested dice for this game are 12, 11, 10, 6, 8, 7, and 15, 13, 5, 9, 2, 4.

5. *Roll a pair of dice and the smaller number is subtracted from the larger number. Suggested dice are 20, 18, 16, 15, 12, 10 and 10, 8, 6, 5, 4, 17.

6. *Make one of the numerals on the die a negative number. When -5 is rolled, the player must give three 1-blocks back to the banker. Suggested die for Race for 200 could be 20, -5, 25, 15, 21, 18.

7. Make the race game with multiplication. Roll a pair of dice, and the answer from multiplying the two dice is the amount of blocks the player receives from the banker. Suggested dice are 0, 1, 2, 3, 4, 5 and 2, 3, 4, 5, 6, 10.

8. Play the race game with division. The larger number is the dividend and the smaller number is the divisor. Suggested dice are 24, 24, 48, 48, 12, 12 and 2, 3, 6, 2, 3, 6. These dice are chosen because there are no blocks left over. When different

numerals are selected for the dice and there are remainders, the leftover blocks go to the opponent.

9. Play with add, subtract, multiply, and divide. The first suggested die is +, −, x, x, ÷, ÷. The other two suggested dice are 2, 3, 4, 5, 6, 8 and 12, 16, 20, 25, 30, 36. Leftovers go to the opponent. With these dice, players will receive more blocks than with other games, so play Race to 500 or even higher.

10. *Up the difficulty by playing Race for 1,000. Sample numbers on the die could be 27, 72, 120, 102, 80, 48. Generally this game is introduced in first grade.

11. Use play money to play Race for a Million Dollars. Sample dice could be $100,000; $111,111; $150,000; $85,000; $50,000; $75,000.

Measurement

12. *Race for a Week. Students trade in 24 hours (two 10-blocks and four 1-blocks) for an object labeled "Sunday." Students gather days until one player is able to trade seven days for "One Week."

Figure 10.2

13. *Race for a Day. Students trade in 60 minutes (utilizing blocks) for an item labeled "one hour." The winner is the first person to trade in 24 hours for a day. Sample die could be 1 hour, 2 hours, 30 minutes, 2 ½ hours, 1 ½ hours, 90 minutes.

14. Race for a Square Yard. Students roll a die for square feet or a fractional part of a square foot. Cut square feet from cardboard so that the winner is the first one to place 9 square feet into a 3-by-3 square to make a square yard. Sample die could be 1 sq. ft., ½ sq. ft., ¾ sq. ft., 1½ sq. ft., 1¼ sq. ft., ¼ sq. ft.

15. Race for a Meter. This is almost like Race for a 100-block except a meterstick is placed on a table, and each player lines up their blocks on the left or the right side of the meterstick. Sample die could be 5 cm, 10 cm, 12 cm, 15 cm, 8 cm, 6 cm.

16. Race for a 5-gallon can. Students roll dice and receive actual cups and pints, which they trade up for quarts and gallons. The winner is the first person to trade 5 gallons for the 5-gallon can. Sample die could be 8 cups, 3 cups, 1 pint, 1 quart, 2 quarts, 1 gallon.

17. *Race for a Year. Students roll dice and trade 31 in blocks for January, then 28 blocks for February, etc. Gather up two calendars and give each player one month from their calendar until the winner has received all 12 months. Sample die could be 31 days, 30 days, 50 days, 70 days, 20 days, 25 days.

Fractions

18. Even at age 5, children can play the race fraction games. Divide up circles, squares, rectangles, etc. into fraction pieces. Label each of the pieces as ⅓, ¼, etc. Young children can match the fraction of the die with the label on the fraction piece. Usually, this is played with the winner being the first person to trade for five tortillas, five chocolate bars, or five waffles. Sample die for Race for Tortillas could be ¼, 1/3, 1/6, ½, 1, 2.

Figure 10.3 Race for Tortillas

19. Every game can be made harder by adjusting the fractions. Change the die from ⅓ to ⅔, for example. There is no piece labeled ⅔, so children learn this means to pick up two of the ⅓ pieces.

20. *Race for a day with 10-year-olds can be very challenging when the numerals on the die are ⅔ day, 1 5/6 day, ⅞ day, ¾ day, 2¼ days, 11/12 day.

Final Thoughts on Games

- ✦ Math games should be so powerful they are the assignment.
- ✦ Remember to approximate about 10 rolls of the dice for each player before there is a winner.
- ✦ The adult continually stretches the knowledge of the children by adjusting the numerals on the dice.
- ✦ These games take the guess work out of so much future math learning. Children see that math is really trading with whole numbers, measurement, and fractions.

Race games are a huge hit in our house. First, they don't feel like school. Since I normally do most of the formal education in our house, this is a fun way to get my husband involved. We always save the race games for Dad to do when he gets home. It allows him to have fun with the kids when he gets home from work while also allowing him an opportunity to be a part of their education. These games have been huge for teaching regrouping. When I tried to teach the regrouping on paper the way I was taught, my oldest son got frustrated and wanted to stop. The moment it became a game (and a race!), he was invested, and the regrouping happened much more naturally with intrinsic motivation still in place. It took a lot of re-teaching me that worksheets, drills, and tricks don't equal knowledge.

*These race games and most other race games require the use of base ten blocks. The games with an * by them are included with the purchase from Amazon of *How to Create a Math Foundation for Future Math Experts*. The package includes all necessary items except for the base ten blocks. This includes the dice, stickers for the dice, and special items for Race for a Week, Race for a Year, and Race for a Day.

CHAPTER 11

This Is Huge: Whole Number and Fraction Computation

"No one is good at doing something new. Get over it."

John Maxwell

There are two basic methods for teaching mathematics:

+ Teach rules and have children practice over and over until they can complete the computation with the prescribed rules.

+ Teach the mathematics with simple understanding so the processes are understood with tools first, then gradually move on to pencil and paper alone.

In support of the second method, there are six books written for mathematics understanding included in The Perfect School Collection™ located on Amazon under Lyle Lee Jenkins.

Several years ago, I saw the data from a sixth-grade standardized exam in an affluent school district. Ninety percent of the sixth graders missed $1/5 \div 1/5 =$ _____ and $\frac{1}{2} \div \frac{1}{4} =$ _____. The students were told how to divide fractions by inverting the divisor, multiplying, and reducing to lowest terms. Obviously, they did not remember the rule. The sad truth is no rule is needed for this problem. Any number divided by itself has an answer of 1. The children know that $3 \div 3 = 1$, but were never taught about this same idea for fractions. Further, if the children were asked how many $\frac{1}{4}$'s are in $\frac{1}{2}$, they would know there are two $\frac{1}{4}$'s in a half. They were not taught what the question means—only a rule to be memorized.

As a child I struggled with math. I may have received A's and B's on my report card, but that wasn't because I truly understood what I was doing. My goal was to memorize formulas long enough to write them at the top of my test and perform well enough so that I wouldn't let down my teacher or parents. The math never clicked for me, and I remember always feeling anxious about having to remember things past the tests I took. Or I had a fear that I'd never be able to use a calculator in everyday life. Yes, that's right, the feelings I had surrounding math were anxiety and fear. That stayed with me through adulthood, and I attribute that to the tricks and formulas I memorized because I did not have a solid mathematical foundation. I want better for my children!

As I read what Kelly wrote, I am reminded of what Dr. W. Edwards Deming taught. He stated there are two kinds of problems: special and common. Kelly thought her frustration with math was a special problem that very few people had. However, she described a very common problem faced by most people. Every time we are faced with a problem, we need to ask ourselves, "Is this a common problem or a special problem?" If it is common, then the problem is most often the system and not the individual. In Kelly's case, the problem was common—a dislike and struggle memorizing all those rules. If it is a special problem, it could be the individual and not a problem with the system at large.

I estimate from hundreds of conversations with adults that half of them do not know that square roots have anything to do with squares. Here is a first-grade problem: What is the square root of 9? The directions are to pick up nine 1-blocks and arrange them into a square shape. Count how long the sides are and write the answer of 3. Tell the children we should change the term "square root" to "square sides"; it would make so much more sense. For fun, here is another easy square-root problem for youngsters: What is the square root of 441? The directions are to pick up four 100-blocks, four 10-blocks, and one 1-block. Arrange them into a square and count the length of the sides.

This student is just starting third grade in a home school. His first square-root problem is to find the square root of 441.

Figure 11.1 Square Root of 441

Figure 11.2

The example in this chapter demonstrates the ease with which all elementary math with whole numbers can be understood with an amazing invention, base ten blocks.

Figure 11.3

The book *How to Create Math Experts with Base Ten Blocks* includes directions for estimating the square root of numbers that do not make an even square. For example, "What is the square root of 10? 11? 12?"

The major focus of the book is for children to learn how to compute addition, subtraction, multiplication, and division first with blocks, then without them. Along the way, children learn the use of these math operations: one addition concept, two subtraction concepts, two multiplication concepts, and three division concepts.

Another book in the series is *How to Create Math Experts with Fraction Slices.* Pick up any education supply catalog and skip to the fraction section. Almost all the materials teach what a fraction is, but then the +, −, x, ÷ are taught with rules to memorize rather than tools for grasping the meaning of the concepts. Adults are amazed at the deep understanding children obtain from the *Fraction Slices* book.

Fraction Slices *have helped my kids visually compare each fraction. They love working with them. A direct quote from my second-grade son is, "They are fun to use and I love their colors!" Not long after working with fraction slices, my son was able to add fractions in his head. It surprised and delighted me!*

Figure 11.4

Translucent fraction slices are physical objects that allow students to learn with a hands-on approach. The fraction slices are superior to other fraction materials because of the ease they bring to understanding addition, subtraction, multiplication, and division with fractions.

Home educators will be amazed at the fraction computation children will be able to do in their heads after completing *How to Create Math Experts with Fraction Slices.*

Another book in the series is *How to Create Math Experts with the Math Balance.* The math balance is a balance scale that includes numerals from 1 to 10 on both the left and right sides.

Home educators could begin with division for very young children because it is easy to solve with the math balance. Take the problem 8 ÷ 2 = _____. The process is to place a weight on the 8 on the left side, then count how many weights on the 2 are needed for the math balance to balance with equal value on both sizes of the scale.

Figure 11.5

Whenever I bring out the math scale, my kids' eyes open wide and they squeal with excitement. It's so simple, yet still a favorite tool. I remember my kindergartner had zero interest in completing a paper with math problems on it. In fact, he pretended to know nothing to get out of the assignment. (That is his go-to response for anything he doesn't want to do.) Then I set the math scale out and suddenly, he was invested. He completed the assignment quickly when minutes before he had "no idea" what the answers were.

The math expert books are written to challenge children of all ages. The QR code in each book provides a download of all student pages for duplication. One set of tools and books can be used for the whole family with no need to purchase materials yet again.

CHAPTER 12

Geometry and Measurement: So Much Fun

"We must preserve the power of intrinsic motivation, dignity, cooperation, curiosity, joy in learning, that people are born with."

W. Edwards Deming

Three geometry books are available in The Perfect School Collection™ located on Amazon under Lyle Lee Jenkins. They are *How to Create Math Experts with Pattern Blocks*, *How to Create Math Experts with Tangrams*, and *How to Create Math Experts with Geoblocks*.

All the math books in The Perfect School Collection™ are designed to be copied and utilized with all children in the family. The investment in the books and the accompanying math materials is a one-time expense that will last for many years and through the education of multiple children.

This is another one of my favorite parts of The Perfect School Collection™. One of the biggest challenges when we started our home-school journey was the cost associated with curriculum. We primarily live on one income. There were very few options affordable to us, and it was hard because the ones that were affordable couldn't be used for multiple children. With The Perfect School Collection™, I love that I can have all three of my children using the same tools and books for K-6th without having to pay three separate fees. In addition, I feel more confident that they are gaining the knowledge they need to be successful! Before I was going through lessons to check them off our list. Now I am checking off skills once I know the children have learned them.

Six sets of tangrams are recommended for use over several years.

Two sets of pattern blocks are ample, and one set of Geoblocks is required.

The criteria for selecting each of these math materials is mathematical. Each of the seven tangram pieces has a relationship with each other piece. The same is true for the 330 pieces in the Geoblocks. All the pieces are mathematically similar to every other piece. The pattern blocks have six different blocks with the same pattern. Each block has a mathematical connection with each of the other blocks.

Figure 12.1

How to Create Math Experts with Pattern Blocks has assignments that will be easy for 4- and 5-year-old children and difficult enough to stump both adults and children ages 10–12. The six sections of the book are Getting Acquainted with the Blocks, Equations, Strategy, Symmetry, Measurement, and Fractions.

When children have the solid foundation provided by the race games, and once they have completed the math books in the How to Create Math Experts series, they will know more mathematics than 99% of their peers.

A set of Geoblocks includes 7 rectangular prisms, 12 triangular prisms, 4 cubes, and 1 pyramid. All the blocks have a mathematical connection to each other.

Figure 12.2

For example, the largest rectangular prism can be built with pyramids, cubes, smaller rectangular prisms, and even triangular prisms. Fascinating! The assignments in *How to Create Math Experts with Geoblocks* explore volume, surface area, ratio, congruence, and geometric relationships.

How to Create Math Experts with Tangrams provides children assignments with 90-degree and 45-degree objects, while *How to Create Math Experts with Pattern Blocks* includes assignments with 30-degree, 60-degree, and 120-degree objects. Again, each of the seven tangrams has a geometric relationship with each of the other pieces. The assignments include geometry, geography, fractions, and examples of 16-base measurements such as in music and liquid measurement, plus a simple introduction to the Pythagorean Theorem.

All the Math Expert books are written with directions and pages to be duplicated for children to

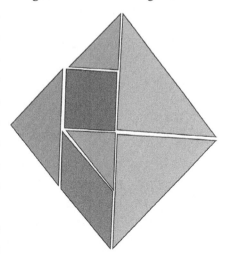

Figure 12.3

record what they learned from the blocks. Only one copy of each book is necessary for a family. In each book is a QR code for downloading student pages from each of the books. The reason for that is the books are made for copying, but copying a book page by page on a copier is tedious. So, the QR code download provides educators with pages ready for copying. The directions are not included in the download; they are in the book already and do not need to be copied.

I love that these books offer a wide variety of ways to practice math using different tools. The discoveries they allow for are much more genuine and exciting than when the children are taught tricks without knowing the "why." My 3-year-old has been able to sit at the table using the same book as my kindergartner and second grader. It's so cool to see!

CHAPTER 13

Music and Art: Do Not Let This Natural Love Die!

*"We ignore the real diamonds of simplicity, seeking
instead the illusory rhinestones of complexity."*

John Bogle

The evidence that intrinsic motivation is being preserved in both art and music is statements beginning with "I can." Every chapter in *How to Create a Perfect Home School* begins with a clear understanding of what preserving intrinsic motivation looks like for a particular subject or skill.

It is well understood that kindergartners believe they can sing, create art, dance, and make up a world of make-believe theatre. Keeping this confidence alive is the aim for children and their home educators. There are children who make it obvious at 5 years old they are determined to excel in the arts. For those children, the aim doubles to include not squelching this drive along with providing more opportunities to develop their talent.

An excellent complete resource for music and other fine arts can be found at musicinourhomeschool.com. The structure and outline of courses therein can provide much guidance for home educators with or without a music background. The ideas below may trigger plans for including more of the arts in the home-school structure:

- Begin with classical music playing in the background before birth and continuing during the home-school time is a very easy way to bring music to children's environment.

73

- The reading section of *How to Create a Perfect Home School* includes instruction on how to have children write or dictate to an adult about art. The same is true for the songs children make up. Record them as text for children to read.

- Compliments go a long way to preserving the "I can." Children need to hear, "You are so good at _____ that you could become a _____."

Choirs in many communities meet once a week for home-school students. Home educators want their children to interact with other children. Some of this time can be like a school recess—only play. However, the interaction from learning together is not to be forgotten, and a home-school choir is an excellent choice.

Lakeshorelearning.com has more than 100 music items for sale: drums, rain sticks, 15-player rhythm sets, tambourines, xylophones, hand bells, etc. Beginning harmonicas and keyboards with lessons are also available.

There are several wonderfully illustrated songbooks. *The Star-Spangled Banner* by Peter Spier is but one of many titles where the whole book includes illustrations line by line from the song.

Be sure to look at books by Floyd Cooper. I have watched him work; he is amazing. He paints the paper a deep dark brown and then does all his drawing with erasers. When the drawing is done, he adds color. Who knows how many children will like Floyd's unusual process for creating art?

Keeping art alive can include no limit to the amount of paper a child has to draw on. Collect paper printed on one side only!

- The internet has a vast number of sites found by searching for "How to Draw a _____." These are so valuable for children because their ability to draw something that is recognizable contributes greatly to the attitude of "I can."

- Books about famous artists and musicians should be in the home-school library.

+ Do not overlook 3-D art. With the invention of cameras in phones, it is so easy to take a picture of the child's 3-D art and print it.

+ A home-school group lesson can easily be created by inviting an artist to come and teach. The group is probably smaller than the choir suggested above, but nevertheless this is a group-learning experience home-school students need.

+ The art in picture books is usually superb for children to emulate. The collages from Eric Carle, the works of various artists selected by Bill Martin Jr., the cartoons by Jim Chansler, the pencil drawings by Tom Wrightman, and the watercolors by Todd Jenkins are all there for children to emulate.

All of these are great options. We spend a lot of time watching tutorials on YouTube and have even paid for a monthly online art lesson subscription. It's all been beneficial, but by far the thing that has encouraged my children's art has been accessibility of supplies. Paper, markers, colored pencils, crayons, etc. are always available. Many times, the children draw and feel compelled to create stories about their art.

Far too often in classrooms I observe one wall displaying students' art and across the room a display of their writing. Then after students have heard a book read, they leave their classroom to go to a music lesson. All of these by themselves, writing, art, literature, and music, are wonderful. However, it is not necessary to always separate the subjects. Students writing about their art and listening to a book followed by singing a favorite song can become seamless, integrated learning experiences. Give the direct instruction in specific content, then follow up with as much exploratory freedom as possible. Find a song about the science, use the historical characters as art, or write a play by personifying the math blocks. In most adult jobs, people are carrying out their responsibilities by combining all their knowledge from various subjects and experiences. Children can experience this interdisciplinary learning most of their time in home school.

Art and music are vital to our home. We always have music playing, and our school table is always covered in markers and creations my kids have made that day.

I suggest that children have available a diary-type book labeled, "My Writing Book by _____." The purpose is for children to record emotions—happiness, anger, sadness, jealousy, love, and so on. It is common for teachers to have a student journal for classrooms. Teachers then set a time for children to write in their journal. However, not every child has some emotion running around in their mind at the same time. So, I suggest having the blank book available when needed. Emotion is often connected to the arts, so have the journal ready when needed.

I would expand on this to include Dr. Jenkins' idea of the "do-nothing chair." When my children are feeling a lot of emotions and not ready (or willing) to participate in school, they're welcome to sit in the do-nothing chair. We chose a chair where our school table is visible and there is nothing fun to do nearby. They can choose to sit in the do-nothing chair until they are ready to come back and join school. The chair is not a punishment, it is a choice: either school with a good attitude, or the do-nothing chair until you're ready for school with a good attitude. Sometimes it's good to have a few minutes to zone out.

CHAPTER 14

Science: Keeping the "Why" Alive

*"I was built to endure in a day when beauty
and solidarity went hand in hand."*

Agatha Christie

Home educators will be successful with science instruction when their children keep their "why" alive. This is the verbal clue that the intrinsic motivation for science is thriving. At the age of 2, the incessant "why, why, why" drives many parents crazy. Often it is because adults do not know the answer to the "why" question. Now the children are older, and "why" seems to drift off. Please encourage these questions! Here are a few suggestions for dealing with the barrage. The aim is to learn together along with your children. I have yet to meet a parent who knows the answers to every "why" question from their children.

Keeping this "why" alive is the challenge, and at the same time the foundation, for science learning. Here are suggestions for responses to yet another "why" question:

1. I know why, and I will explain soon.

2. I don't know why, and nobody knows why.

3. I don't know why, but I know somebody who does know why. We will ask together.

4. I don't know why, but I believe we can learn from an internet or library search. Then if we want to know more, we will visit the library to find a book.

5. I don't know why because there are so many different opinions.

The previous part of this chapter could be labeled "science from following children's curiosity." What follows are suggestions for building more science foundation through adult-led activities instead of child-led learning. Some suggestions follow; use the ones that seem most helpful.

1. Classification

Scientists have developed a classification system to keep science knowledge organized. The major categories are physical, life, and earth science. The major categories within each are:

1. Physical science is natural objects studied in physics, chemistry, and astronomy.

2. Life science is plants, animals, and very small objects seen only with a microscope.

3. Earth science is our planet's physical attributes such as earthquakes, floods, fossils, and the atmosphere.

When children are young, certain concepts can spur deep thinking if the children are given space to explore. For example, the distinction between alive and not alive is hard. It can create deep thinking on the child's part if the parent is not too eager to teach. Here's a classification conversation inspired by the research of Jean Piaget:

Adult: Is this cat alive?
Child: Yes.
Adult: How do you know?
Child: The cat moves.
Adult: Oh, so that is how you know if things are alive or not—if they move. Right?
Child: Yes.
Adult: What about this clock. It moves. Is it alive?
Child: (Confused look is most likely.)

Adult: Think about what is alive and let me know what you think after a while.

It is so hard for parents to let this go. Why? Children do figure out why the clock is not alive on their own. Patience is required. Parents can ask later, "Is the car alive? It moves." When children are told answers they are not logically ready for, they invent reasons why what the adult said is true. These reasons then need to be unlearned. It is better to help the child's reasoning by asking more intriguing questions.

Classification is very important in the structure of science. Most often, people classify with matrix diagrams or Venn diagrams. The matrix looks like this:

Science Measurement Matrix

	Length	Width	Height	Weight	Area	Volume
Bearded Dragon	36cm	6cm	8cm	160g	105cm²	
Toothbrush	22cm	2.5cm	2.5cm	120g		100ml
T-Rex Toy				30g		
Mandalorian Toy	15cm	5.5cm	3cm	70g		
Miniature Pumpkin	9.5cm	9.5cm	4.5cm	260g	48.5cm²	

Figure 14.1

The matrix is a superb way for people to visualize all they have accomplished.

I would label images with names for each column and row. Items have only one cell on the matrix where they can be placed. A Venn diagram is different in that items can belong in several categories. In the Venn diagram, if one circle is labeled red, the second one blue, and the third one white, the flag of the USA is placed in the center because it belongs in all three circles at once. The flag of Ukraine fits only in the blue circle because it is blue and yellow.

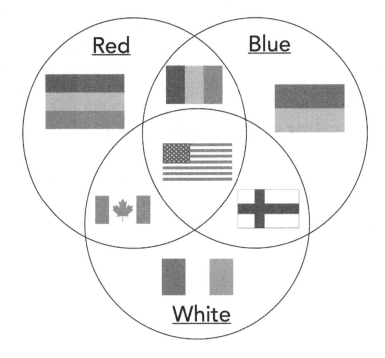

Figure 14.2

Buttons are a great activity for children to classify with a Venn diagram. Label each of the three circles with an attribute such as "plastic," "2 holes," and "red." Then place the buttons where the classification is correct. Some buttons, like one that is wooden, black, and has four holes, will be off to the side.

Environment

The environment can be large, such as the Sonoran Desert, smaller such as a park, or very small such as a square meter or yard. The idea is to become very good at making observations and recording them. The square meter can change quite a bit throughout the year as seasons come and go. I suggest studying the local environment, such as the Sonoran Desert where the two authors live. Children should have a three-ring binder labeled, for example, "The Sonoran Desert Encyclopedia." Inside will be a set of alphabet dividers. As children complete work, it is filed away after the correct letter tab.

The work is edited by the home educator for spelling, punctuation, and capitalization while the student author listens. The changes may be entered into a word processor and printed out. Laminate the pages sometimes but always punch three holes in them. Students build upon the encyclopedia, and it lasts for multiple years. The only change is that a second binder may be needed, so one encyclopedia would have the first half of the alphabet and the other binder the second half.

We absolutely love our Sonoran Desert encyclopedia. Every week my kids choose something from the desert to research (petrified wood, javelina, McDowell Mountains, etc.). My second grader writes five sentences about the topic, and my kindergartner writes three facts. They spend a great deal of time choosing their topic and learning about it. Afterward, they love the finished product because it's laminated in their book that they can read and re-read. It is so fun!

Hands-On Activities

Children can use simple household items that come from the grocery or hardware store to conduct experiments and record the data. I am giving examples from a book that is now out of print entitled *Kitchen Physics*. These examples will give home educators the structure for children to conduct experiments by changing only one item at a time. Use the word "variable" with the children. Everything stays constant in the experiments except one item that becomes the variable. The variable changes, and the children record the result of the change.

Keeping the will and thrill alive for science depends upon hands-on activities like these:

1. Put 5 drops of water on various surfaces and draw what you see. The 5 drops is the constant; the surfaces of plastic, wood, tile, aluminum foil, glass, and waxed paper are the variables.

2. Drop various liquids onto a solid surface. The solid surface is the constant. The variables are water, soapy water, vinegar, rubbing alcohol, and cooking oil. Draw what you see with each variable. Label everything.

3. Fill a very small container with water. The container could be the size of one used for medicine. Fill it as far as possible without spilling. Then use a medicine dropper to drop single drops of water onto the top until it spills. Count the number of drops and record adjacent to the word "water" on the recording paper. Repeat this experiment with soapy water, vinegar, rubbing alcohol, and cooking oil. Each liquid will have a different surface tension. The constant is the amount of liquid; the variable is the different liquids.

4. Find a solid slick surface about the size of a sheet of paper and 4 medicine droppers. Fill each of them with water, soapy water, alcohol, or cooking oil. Four people stand behind the solid surface, which is slanted slightly. At a set time, each person squeezes out all the liquid in their medicine dropper. Which liquid wins the race to the bottom of the slanted solid surface? The constant is the amount of liquid; the variable is the different liquids.

5. Dip 5 sheets of paper towel into 5 different liquids: water, soapy water, vinegar, rubbing alcohol, and cooking oil. Dip each paper towel the same amount into the liquid. Hang the 5 paper

towels up on a coat hanger. Time how long it takes each paper towel to dry completely. The constant is the amount of liquid in the paper towel; the variable is the different liquids.

History

The history of science is very interesting to many children. The resources are multiple and varied from books to media. Items that we take for granted like telephones, computers, electricity, refrigerators, engines, and even toilets all have a history. None of these were always available. Encourage children to explore the origins of these household items.

Measurement

When children have the opportunity to measure whatever they desire, their interest often goes to science. We suggest that these activities be completed with metric measurements because metric is used in science.

Measure weight. Use a pan balance with metric weights. The larger weights should be at least 500 grams, but preferably a kilogram. Children select what they want to weigh and record it. This Bearded Dragon weighs 53 grams, for example.

Figure 14.3

Measure length. The question might be, "How long is the longest python?" A big collection of donated rulers helps this activity. The child finds out that the longest python is 30 feet long. He takes out 30 rulers and places them end to end and cuts a piece of yarn the same length. Then, he uses a meterstick to see the equivalent length. He saves these lengths.

The bearded dragon was quite calm while his length and width were being measured.

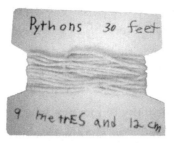

Figure 14.4

Figure 14.5

Figure 14.6

Measure volume. Be sure to have a liter container that is graduated so children can easily count milliliters. Students used a graduated liter tube to find the volume of a toothbrush.

Figure 14.7

Measure area. Base ten blocks are metric, so it will be easy to approximate the area of items around the house. The bearded dragon was placed on centimeter graph paper and traced. Then students counted each square centimeter and placed a check mark in each partial square centimeter. They counted each partial square centimeter as ½ cm².

All the above ideas are to help home educators keep the "why" alive in elementary school. There is ample time to learn a great deal of science in years to come. When the "why" is kept alive, students are ready to dig in depth in aspects of science that are particularly interesting.

Figure 14.8

Resources for science include:

1. Children need a good science dictionary written for them.

2. NGSS stands for Next Generation Science Standards. On the internet, teachers can find a multitude of materials organized by grade levels. K–2 and 3–5 are the age spans for the audience of this book.

3. EAIeducation.com has many science resources available, including books and equipment. The organization is for ages 4–6, 6–8, 8–10, and 10–12. Also, the products can be searched by price range.

The beauty of homeschooling is that we can be intentional about the whys our children ask. We have the time to allow them to explore in the kitchen without hurrying onto the next thing. I do not recall a time when I was allowed to explore my own interests in the way my children are able to through home school. Giving them this flexibility is a joy to watch. Do not underestimate the value of baking with your children, along with making mistakes. I tend to remind my children (and myself) that failure is a great teacher. I love that we have time to fail!

CHAPTER 15

Loving History and Geography

"Learning can be defined as 'the process of developing sufficient surface knowledge to then move to deeper understanding such that one can appropriately transfer this learning to new tasks and situations.'"

Douglas Fisher, Nancy Frey, and John Hattie

For elementary-age students, the most important social studies subjects are history, geography, and local civics and places. Each of these three has suggested opportunities for home-school families. The aim is as true for history, geography, and local as it is for all other aspects of education: keep the intrinsic motivation alive for all our children, and the learning will come easily. There is no reason for children to develop a dislike for any of the social studies content. I suggest that home educators use the vocabulary "history," "geography," and "civics," and the actual names of places they visit rather than the generic term "social studies."

I cannot tell readers how many adults I have met who have said, "I hated history when I was in school, but I really love history now—both books and documentaries." None of these adults told me they went online to purchase a new copy of History 101. Why the change in attitude? It could be maturity, but I do not think so. It is because the adults can explore an area of interest in detail as opposed to skimming a multitude of topics. Examples from my own reading are *Longitude: The Story of a Lone Genius Who Solved the Greatest Scientific Problem of His Time* by Dava Sobel and William J.H. Andrewes, and *On Wings Like Eagles: The Last Days of Dietrich Bonhoeffer* by Ben Clevenger.

History

For elementary-age children, home educators have three major responsibilities:

1. Keep the love of learning about times past alive.

2. Integrate the Bible and Christian history with societal history.

3. Give elementary-age children hundreds of reasons to be proud of the heritage of the United States. There will be ample time in later years to learn about the serious wounds some Americans have inflicted upon our country.

I was absolutely the one who left school thinking history was boring. Apart from two teachers in my entire school career, it always felt boring. It never felt relevant. Now, however, documentaries and personal stories are fascinating, and I cannot get enough. The history that captivated me as an adult has captivated my children at an early age, and I am so grateful. We read about people and learn their stories. We connect them to the other stories we have learned. Did you ever know growing up that the T. rex did not live at the same time as the Brachiosaurus? Well, I did not, and it shattered my ideas about dinosaurs (but not until I was 30 and learning this alongside my children). My point is, I want my children to realize that, for example, Abraham Lincoln was a wonderful president who issued the Emancipation Proclamation in 1863. That was a huge step forward. However, it was 100 years later that Martin Luther King Jr. gave his famous "I Have a Dream" speech. No, the T. rex did not live alongside the Brachiosaurus, and there were also many years between that important document and that important speech. The time line creates a way for us to connect our history together. It also creates empathy. We read about Mozart, and by the end of the book, my children were referring to him as "Wolfie." They loved knowing his story. That led them to want to listen to more classical music, which they did. That also led them to create more music. History is so much more than a book of events; it is about human stories and the way they come together. Our time line is like a scrapbook of stories we have come to appreciate and understand in a meaningful way.

One tool of great value for accomplishing all three responsibilities is a time line from 2000-plus BC to current times. This is something the students will create. The reason this is so important is that children can study historical events that greatly interest them in a random sequence based upon interests. Placing notes on the home-school time line gives children the sense of history that chronological textbooks are designed to do. For example, some children will be interested in using a compass. Then they may want to know the history of the compass. They can read the book *Compass: A Story of Exploration and Innovation* by Alan Gurney. In the Bible's book of Acts, Paul wintered in various cities in the first century. The reason for wintering was because the ships did not sail on the Mediterranean Sea in the winter because of cloud cover; sailors couldn't see the stars and know their location. Once the compass was discovered in the 1300s, ships sailed most of the year. This allowed merchants in Venice to greatly increase their income. If this history interests children, they can place a note on the time line to remind them how this fits into the overall history of the world. We can follow children's interest without a boring quick summary of every event.

When children read books about the Bible, such as the early reader *A Very Long Day with Elijah: The Contest* by Lyle Lee Jenkins, they can search on the internet to learn that Elijah lived between 900 and 999 BC. The students can record this information on the time line along with nonbiblical information such as Aesop lived in the century from 500 to 599 BC.

Obviously, many people live in two centuries. Usually, the later century will be where the information is placed on the time line.

A family may have a lot of space dedicated to homeschooling only. In that case, the family may want to place a time line on the wall around the room like a teacher would do in a regular classroom. For most home schools, a physical time line on the wall is impractical. I recommend an accordion time line, which is a hardcover do-it-yourself scrapbook folding photo album in two packs. Appendix M, which shows centuries and time periods, can be printed on templates for printing with 32 labels. There is history in every subject—science, Christianity, art, music, athletics, and inventions as simple as a safety pin.

When the US Congress passed the No Child Left Behind law in 2002, an unintended consequence was that the fifth-grade history of the United States was eliminated in most schools. When people are told to raise reading test scores or risk being fired, the natural inclination is to triple the time spent teaching reading and eliminate other content. The biggest elimination was history, followed by geography, science, and in extreme cases, even recess. Not only did this misguided legislation and subsequent fallout fail to improve reading, but teaching for patriotism and history was greatly reduced. The foundation for the creation of a democracy when the world was controlled by kings must be understood and appreciated. Home educators can be leaders in restoring US history to its rightful place in the curriculum.

One of the very best ways for children to learn about US history is through picture books. Hundreds of beautifully illustrated historical picture books give so much detail through both the art and the text. Invest in these, and children will read them over and over. Then have children select a favorite part of the book to illustrate and write about. Two example books are *Paul Revere's Ride* illustrated by Ted Rand, and *How They Built the Statue of Liberty* by Mary J. Shapiro.

The following two examples of children's reflections upon the experience with a history picture book were created with tangrams and pattern blocks.

Home educators have the responsibility and joy of infusing biblical and Christian history along with many other worldwide events. Students record artistic accomplishments alongside Christian events seamlessly. For example, in the 300s Christian leaders agreed upon which books and letters would be included in the Bible's New Testament. These historical events all fit on the home-school accordion time line.

This is the church
Paul Revere hung
the two lanterns.And
one lantern means
they are coming by
land and if two lanters are up
it means they are coming by water.

Figure 15.1

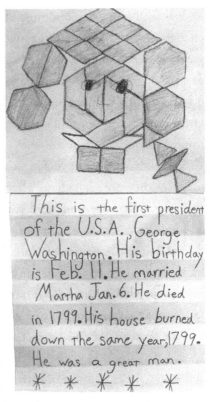

This is the first president
of the U.S.A. George
Washington. His birthday
is Feb. 11. He married
Martha Jan. 6. He died
in 1799. His house burned
down the same year,1799.
He was a great man.
✳ ✳ ✳ ✳ ✳

Figure 15.2

Geography

Geography has six essential elements. For home educators wishing to go beyond the first two, ample resources are available for purchase or free download. However, for *How to Create a Perfect Home School*, only the first two (world spatial terms and places/regions) are included in this chapter. The spatial terms are "equator," "latitude," "longitude," "north pole," "south pole," and so on. The places begin with continents followed by geographical features such as the Andes Mountains or the Sahara, then political boundaries for countries and regions within countries. Mexico and the United States names those regions states, while Canada names them provinces.

It is well known that almost all US citizens struggle with knowing enough geography. Sit in a taxi with a driver who seems to be an immigrant. When you ask where the driver is from, the answer is the name of a country followed, without any pause, describing where the country is located. The immigrant assumes that you are a US citizen and do not know geography. Ten million home-school students can go a long way toward solving this problem.

When having a conversation with new acquaintances, the people may say they are Canadian. They almost never tell you the province. Ask where they are from, and you will not hear, "I'm from Manitoba." You will hear, "I'm from Canada" because they assume that US citizens do not know the names of Canadian provinces. Sadly, the Canadians know the 50 US states far better than the US citizens know Canada's 10 provinces and 3 territories. Ten million home-school students can go a long way toward solving this problem.

Our other neighbor, Mexico, has 31 states plus the capital Mexico City. Most US citizens do not know this, and we rarely hear the names of the states. In Arizona, it is common to see a license plate from the state of Sonora, but that is not so in many other US states. We can do better; ten million home-school students can go a long way toward solving this problem.

I suggest organizing a three-ring binder with dividers labeled for each continent plus one for vocabulary. If the binder has a clear cover to hold a title, I suggest printing a picture of a globe with the heading "Geography: Places and Vocabulary We Know."

When students can find a country on their globe, they are ready to add a page to the collection inside the binder. They can download pictures and write or dictate information for their page. If they meet somebody from that locale, students can interview them. The ideas are endless, but the basic purpose of the binder is to visually document places and regions students can find on the globe. This is basic geography literacy.

An excellent experience for children is to have the app for *The Jesus Film* on a computer or phone. The main video on the app is simply called "Jesus." As of April 2022, the original filming of the story of Jesus has been reposted with voice-overs by native speakers in 1,960 languages. Have children click on the map at the bottom of the app, and they will see places where *The Jesus Film* has a voice-over. West of Africa is Cape Verde. Click on this icon and up will come Portuguese and two other languages spoken in Cape Verde that have the voice-over. Children will not understand what is being said, but when learning about another country, many are interested in hearing the language spoken. Children should listen to *The Jesus Film* first in their native language. Then for fun, they can follow some of the story in another language. Children can learn that understanding the approximately 7,000 languages in the world is not a problem for God.

I also encourage home educators to be aware that the largest building under construction in Africa is the Bible Museum of Africa. Construction is underway in Accra, Ghana. The country of Ghana need not be merely a place on the map of Africa, but a country to follow. Every country in the world has interesting facts about it just like Ghana and the Bible Museum. These details are what make geography so interesting to children and adults.

An internet search for geography games brings up several free apps that can be used for fun learning. It is not that elementary-age children should know every country in the world, but they can know the majority without any struggle. For learning the states, go to LtoJ.net and look under "Free Resources." Click on PowerPoints for Quizzes, then Social Studies, then the 50 States Presentation. The download for the 50 states works well. Open it in slideshow and click on one of the 50 numerals. A map of the United States will come up with one state is highlighted. See whether children know this name, then click on the space bar. The answer appears. Knowing the location of the 50 states is essential knowledge for children growing up in the United States. Knowing the capital of each state is far less important. It is OK for adults to look up the capital of some state and not be embarrassed. However, it is embarrassing for adults to hear the name of a US state and have no clue where it is located. Ten million home-school students can solve this problem.

The moment that made me feel like things were clicking was when my husband went out of town. We live in Arizona, but my husband went to a conference in Oregon. As I've mentioned, my second grader has been studying the states. He explained to me that it comforted him to know that his dad was only two states away, just above California. Then, he proceeded to take a map and measure with his fingers how far Oregon was from Arizona. Knowing that it took two and a half hours to fly to Oregon, he used the distance he just measured to estimate that it would take 17 and a half hours to fly to Antarctica. We decided to check his hypothesis. Lo and behold, he was within an hour! It was incredible to see the transfer of his knowledge that John Hattie outlined for us. He went from surface to deep to transfer learning in such a natural, nonlinear way.

One of the ways our family likes to explore geography is through animals. We have started an "Animals Across the Globe" ABC book. This is like our Sonoran Desert Encyclopedia, but instead we research animals from different parts of the world. We locate where the animals live on the map, print the location out, and continue researching the animal and its habitat. As Dr. Jenkins always says, "Find what gets your child's attention and use it to teach."

Local Including Civics

Home educators can also use the ABC book idea for reflection upon civic events. One group of kindergartners studied various occupations, and together they wrote an ABC "Book of Occupations." Following is an image of the cover and one of the pages. "Y" is for yo-yo maker on the page. Without the ABC structure, yo-yo maker would never have occurred to the children. Thus, the slight constraint with ABC books creates unusual creativity. Not all words need to

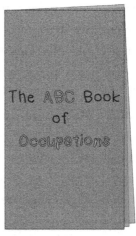

Figure 15.3

begin with the letter itself. For example, I have photos from an ABC "Book of Mathematics" where "J" is for adjacent. Likewise, an ABC "Book of Ancient Egypt" has "X" for Sphinx.

Figure 15.4

I suggest studying how organizations work—governments, business-es, museums, and other agencies such as Habitat for Humanity. Focus on the local so that home-school children can visit a city council meeting, talk to employees at a local museum, and have a tour of a fire station with time to ask questions about the workings of the station. Schedule an appointment with the owner or manager of a business. Remember to focus on how things work because none of what the children see happens with the snap of a finger.

Who paved this street? Who pays for it? Who hired the pavers? What material is used to pave? Where does all this come from? Who mixes it? Who gives permission to pave? Who does the work to pave a highway out in the country? You get the idea. It is just like the science chapter—keep the "why" alive. Add some "who," "how," and "when" to the mix of "why."

For civics, I suggest another three-ring binder with alphabet dividers. The title of the binder can be the name of the place, then "dictionary." An example is, "The Arizona Dictionary of Places, People, Things and Actions."

This need not be work for students—keep it simple! Take photos on a phone during a visit. Decide with students what picture should be printed. Then, the adult sits at the computer to type the thoughts of students in a dictionary format.

1. Word

2. Definition

3. Part of Speech

4. Pronunciation

5. Sentence(s)

Print the dictionary statements with the photos. Use the three-hole punch on the printed page and place the page in the three-ring binder after the correct letter of the alphabet.

This process is important for many reasons, but one is the power of reflection upon learning. It is easy to forget about an experience unless you reflect on it. We might have forgotten about a childhood experience, but because our parents had photos of it and showed the photo to us and many others over the years, we remember the experience. Do we remember the actual experience or the reflection (photograph and discussion)? It doesn't really matter. We remember it. These dictionary statements are reflections. Most schools, when the year is over, discard the materials. With home school, the three-ring binder for their places is not discarded; it is ready and able to accept more entries year after year as the place is explored in more detail.

I know there are many fantastic teachers of history and geography in our schools. I have been in their classrooms, and I am in awe. The issue is that children's experience with social studies in middle school, high school, and college is not as powerful as it should be. I believe this is due to requiring too many survey courses and not the interesting details children love. At one time, I was on the faculty in elementary education at Oregon State University. We changed the requirement for future teachers from taking US History 101 and 102 to taking two semesters of US history. The logic was that students had already completed several survey courses and were ready to develop expertise. The feedback from the students was so positive. We had the same teachers, same students, and same university, but now students were able to dig into details about an aspect of history that really interested them. Home educators can learn from this OSU experience and all the suggestions for history, geography, and local so their children love history all their life.

CHAPTER 16

The Bible: Connecting Branches to the Vine

"There is great joy in gaining the results God desires."

John Maxwell

The climax for *How to Create a Perfect Home School* is this chapter. Jesus said, as recorded in John 15:5, "I am the vine; you are the branches." God's desire is for everyone to have their very best life connected to the vine. The first 15 chapters of *How to Create a Perfect Home School* were designed to assist home educators create the very best branches (their children). Chapter 16 is about connecting our branches to the vine, Jesus. God has great plans in mind for each of our branches; they can come to fruition when they are connected to Jesus. Amazing branches connected to the vine Jesus will accomplish much good for humanity.

Most home-school educators want the Bible taught directly to their children and for biblical events and Christian worldview to be naturally woven into the weekly activities. Let's be more intentional about the indirect, natural infusion of the Bible with the academic content. For example, one early reading practice, described in Chapter 7, is to ask children what word they want to read today. They may ask for a dinosaur word or for "angel" because they recently read *Five Years Protecting Jesus: A Christmas Story* by Lyle Lee Jenkins.

The "web" graphic is the first indirect idea that will work with students at any age with any interest (See Appendix N).

Home educators can enter any topic that interests their children into the center of the Appendix N graphic, and they will find ways to explore the topic. This applies to all school subjects, including the Bible. Students can study each subject as part of an interdisciplinary theme or as a subject by itself. The Bible is no exception; any topic can be connected to the Bible. Literature is an example. The Hebrew form of poetry rhymed thoughts more than sounds. The poet stated a thought and then stated the same thought again with different words. Even if the child is interested in technology, and it seems like no connections are possible, there are always connections. Technology represents recent inventions, and many inventions took place during biblical times including paper, writing surfaces, and written language. Both home educators and their children will be absolutely amazed by the journeys that occur because of this simple web planning device. The web planner is one of the very best ways to teach the Bible indirectly.

A second indirect Bible teaching is through the Bible Patterns for Young Readers series described in Chapter 9. It is obvious that a central purpose of the books is telling children that they can "make a go" of reading as suggested by Bill Martin Jr. However, since the books are based upon Bible stories, there is a great deal of knowledge gained by young children through the learning to read process. Further, each of the books has background knowledge for adults to share with children. There is a reason for the background knowledge. When children's Bible books include all the details, the book becomes too difficult for early readers. When home educators share the background knowledge with children, they are moving on from indirect Bible knowledge to directly teaching the Bible.

How to Create Bible Experts: Genesis to Revelation by Richard Douglas Junior Jenkins has a unique structure for direct teaching of the Bible. This resource is structured for children to study 20 biblical events, then add another 20, so that they are studying 40. Over the years, other sets of 20 are added until all 120 are firmly in children's minds.

One of the exemplary qualities of *How to Create Bible Experts: Genesis to Revelation* is the fun students have placing the events in chronological order. Who lived first, Jonah or Daniel? The answer is not to be achieved through memorization, but by biblical knowledge and context. The book provides chronological markers for adults to share and gives three key points and narrative. Throughout *How to Create a Perfect Home School*, I have made suggestions that integrate biblical knowledge in all academic subjects. It should be natural to include the Bible all along the way, year after year. Secondly, the Bible is a separate school subject to be studied in detail like science, art, or math. I can remember one of my math mentors, Mary Laycock, saying that everywhere she went she saw math. Math was a subject she knew very well, but she also integrated it with all her knowledge beyond math. We desire that our children see God in all aspects of life.

The purpose of Chapter 16 is creating home-school graduates who are well educated in biblical knowledge as well as all the academic school subjects. These children can connect their deep biblical knowledge and insights, for the rest of their life, in all pursuits that God brings into their adult life.

Along with the knowledge of the Bible comes a life of living it out. We have found that the less busy we are, the more intentional we can be with focusing our lives on Him. Homeschooling allows us to fill our schedules how we see fit, but most importantly to fill it first with Jesus. A huge priority for us is our Sabbath. We prepare for our Sabbath as if it is a weekly holiday. If the Creator of our universe rested on the seventh day, then we need that rest even more so! Without a doubt, knowledge and schooling are important, but lifestyle is as well. Our family's goal is to equip our children with academic and biblical knowledge as well as the ability to create a rhythm that allows Jesus to be the center in a world where busyness is king.

Appendices

The appendix items are designed for purchasers of *How to Create a Perfect Home School* to download and utilize with their children. The QR code below will open a dialog box to receive the URL for downloading all the appendix items. These pages are copyrighted, but permission is given to print the ones you need to use with your classroom or home.

The *Will* to Learn
(My Effort)

Will & Thrill

	Not Trying 0%	Some 25%	Coasting 50%	Extra Hard 75%	All of me 100%
Hate					
Dislike					
OK					
Like					
Love					

The *Thrill* of Learning

Will & Thrill Feedback

Helped me work harder:	Helped me enjoy learning more:
This might help us work harder:	Might help us enjoy learning more:

APPENDIX C

Grade 3 - Key Concepts
(Partial List)

Number

1. Round whole numbers to nearest 10,100 or 1000.
2. Fluently add and subtract with two re-groupings.
3. Multiply one-digit numbers.
4. Multiply one-digit numbers by multiples of 10.

    e.g. 9 x 80 =, 5 x 60 =

5. Identify a fractional part of a whole.
6. Represent fractions on a number line.
7. Understand equivalent fractions.
8. Express whole numbers as fractions.

    e.g. 6 = 6/1, 6 = 12/2

9. Compare two fractions with =, < and >.
10. Divide two-digit numbers by one-digit numbers.

Operations and Algebraic Thinking

11. Write word problems for multiplication number sentences.
12. Use three models to represent division concepts: area, share and repeated subtraction.

    Area: if a rectangle has an area of 12 and the width is 3, what is the length?

    Sharing: if there are 12 marshmallows shared by 3 people, how many will each person receive?

    Repeated subtraction: If a person has 12 wheels and wants to make tricycles, how many trikes can they make?

13. Solve multiplication and division problems.
14. Find the missing number in multiplication and division number sentences.
15. Understand associative and distributive properties of multiplication and division.

APPENDIX D

Number of Students

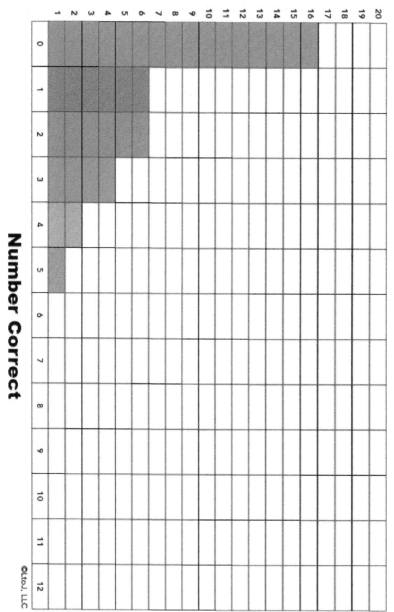

Number Correct

Histogram for Quiz #___1___

APPENDIX E

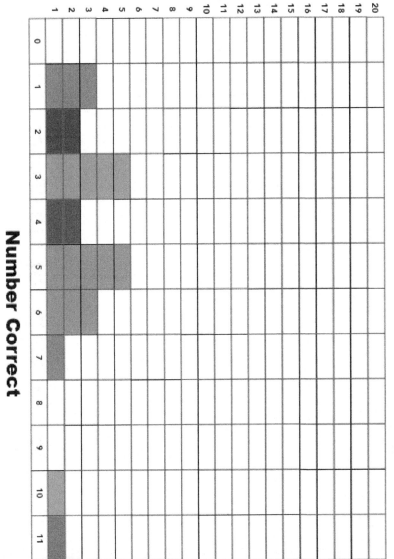

Number of Students

Number Correct

Histogram for Quiz # ___ 15

Number of Students

Histogram for Quiz #___28___

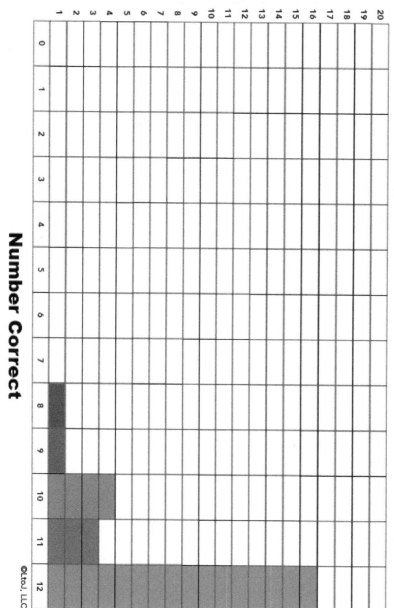

Number Correct

©Ltoj, LLC

APPENDIX G

Number Correct

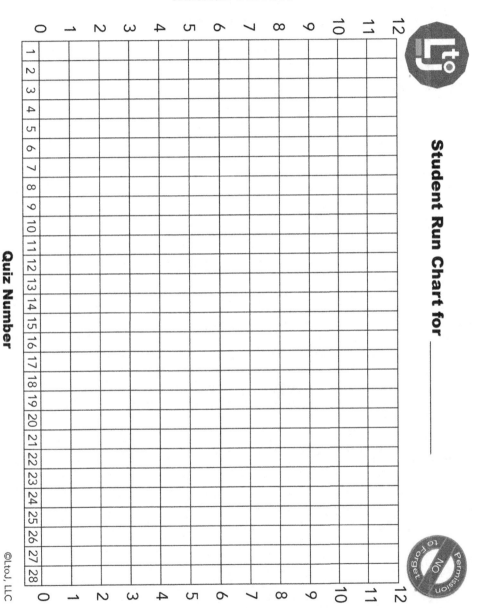

Student Run Chart for _____

Quiz Number

APPENDIX H

Week 1 - Math Standards

Grade 3

Name: _____   **Date:** _____

Grade 1 - Recap: (Standard #21) What's the rule for the shapes inside the circle?	Shapes: Solutions:
Grade 2 - Recap: (Standard #12) Write an addition number sentence for the arrays.	____ + ____ = ____ ____ + ____ + ____ + ____ = ____
Grade 2 - Recap: (Standard #6) Add & Subtract	$\begin{array}{r} 27 \\ +\ 43 \\ \hline \end{array}$ $\begin{array}{r} 70 \\ -\ 27 \\ \hline \end{array}$ $\begin{array}{r} 43 \\ +\ \\ \hline 70 \end{array}$ $\begin{array}{r} 70 \\ -\ \\ \hline 27 \end{array}$
Number (#3) Multiply.	$2 \times 7 =$ $4 \times 7 =$ $8 \times 7 =$
Number (#10) Divide.	$4\overline{)28}\ =$
Number (#5) Name the shaded fraction.	
Number (#8) Place the fraction on the number line.	$\dfrac{3}{3}$ 0 1 2 3 4
Operations & Algebra (#12) What is the division problem?	

Measurement, Data (#26) What is the perimeter of a square with 10cm sides?	**Geometry (#27)** Which quadrilaterals can you make that have 4 equal length sides?

APPENDIX I

12 -6	9 x1	8 +8	15 -5	9 +2	6 x4	17 -10	50 x2	6 +4	34 -3
10 +5	7 x10	14 -6	17 +4	9 x9	3 +3	3 x2	8 -4	17 -7	4 +8
2 x5	25 -10	13 x2	1 +9	19 -3	10 +7	0 x4	16 +5	4 x4	12 -3

111

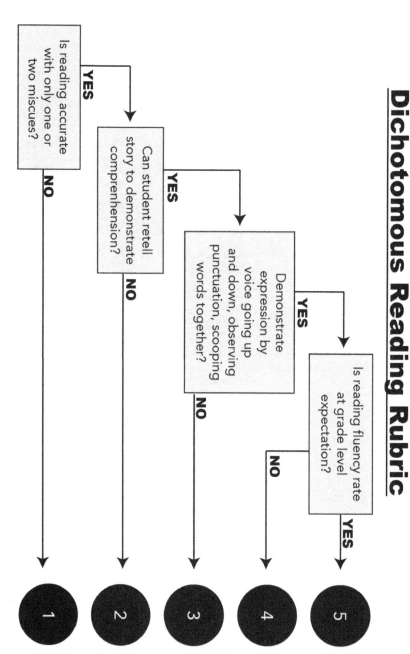

Dichotomous Reading Rubric

Is reading accurate with only one or two miscues?

YES → Can student retell story to demonstrate comprenhension?

NO → 1

YES → Demonstrate expression by voice going up and down, observing punctuation, scooping words together?

NO → 2

YES → Is reading fluency rate at grade level expectation?

NO → 3

NO → 4

YES → 5

APPENDIX K

UPPERCASE - PRINT	Lowercase - Print	UPPERCASE - CURSIVE	Lowercase - Cursive

1. _____

2. _____

3. _____

4. _____

5. _____

6. _____

7. _____

8. _____

9. _____

10. _____

11. _____

12. _____

13. _____

14. _____

15. _____

16. _____

17. _____

18. _____

19. _____

20. _____

21. _____

22. _____

23. _____

24. _____

25. _____

26. _____

27. _____

28. _____

29. _____

30. _____

Create an illustration that pictures 2 or 3 words from above

SENTENCE APPROACHES

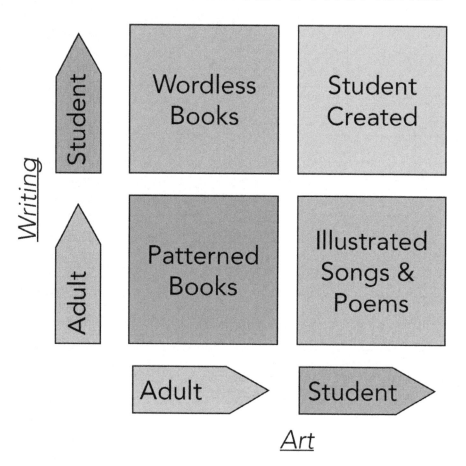

APPENDIX M

2500 BC+	900 - 999
2000 - 2500 BC	1000 - 1099
1500 - 1999 BC	1100 - 1199
1000 - 1499 BC	1200 - 1299
500 - 999 BC	1300 - 1399
0 - 499 BC	1400 - 1499
1 - 50	1500 - 1599
51 - 99	1600 - 1699
100 - 199	1700 - 1799
200 - 299	1800 - 1849
300 - 399	1850 - 1899
400 - 499	1900 - 1949
500 - 599	1950 - 1999
600 - 699	2000 - 2010
700 - 799	2010 - 2020
800 - 899	2020+

APPENDIX N

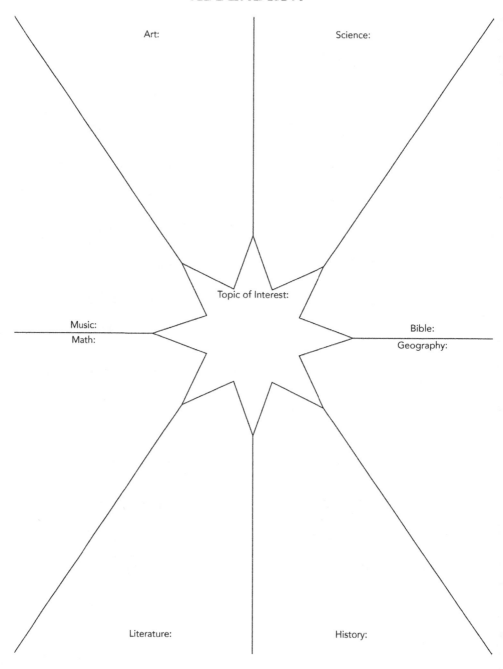

Art:

Science:

Topic of Interest:

Music:
Math:

Bible:
Geography:

Literature:

History:

About the Authors

 **Lyle Lee Jenkins** is an author, speaker, consultant and a recognized expert in improving the systems, outcomes, and processes of education. He is on a mission to provide the training, resources, and encouragement all educators need to help children maintain their intrinsic love of learning.

Lyle Lee holds a Bachelor of Arts degree from Point Loma Nazarene University, a Masters of Education from San Jose State University and a Ph.D. from the Claremont Graduate University. The author of *How to Create Math Experts, How to Create Language Experts, How to Create Bible Experts, Bible Patterns for Young Readers, Aesop Patterns for Young Readers, How to Create a Perfect School* and *How to Create a Perfect Home School*, Lyle Lee has spent the last 50 years learning from teachers, administrators, and world-class experts the best practices for education. During that time, he also worked as a teacher, principal, school superintendent in the California School System, and as a university professor.

Lyle Lee's speaking career has taken him across the U.S. and to many other regions, including Latin America, Europe and Asia. He has taught online courses to educators from more than 25 countries. His message to educators in public, private, charter, and home schools is to promote and maintain the love of learning children were born with throughout all 12 years of school and beyond by celebrating progress, empowering them to own their education, and keeping learning fun. His mission is that every child around the world would have an educational experience that promotes and encourages the intrinsic love of learning that he/she was born with.

Dr. Jenkins would love to hear about your experiences in the field of education. You can contact him at lee@ltoj.net. For free resources and continued education opportunities near you, visit www.ltoj.net.

Kelly Hawkinson Lippert is an author, home educator, and facilitator for home education training. She grew up in Arizona, where she was an educator for fourth and fifth grades before becoming a full-time mother and home school mom. **Kelly attended Fort Hays State University and graduated with a degree in Elementary Education. Active in her local church, she is on the Hospitality team and serves in the church's coffee shop.** Kelly is honored to serve alongside her husband, Cameron, who is the Community Life pastor at their church, and considers her role of pastor's wife as a calling.

One of her greatest privileges is to be a mother to her three amazing children, and she is passionate and thankful for the opportunity to educate them at home. Kelly believes that children were designed to love learning and has a mission to see children all over the world get the opportunities to pursue their God-given creativity without the restraints or hindrances that would diminish that eagerness to learn. *How to Create a Perfect Home School* is her first published book. She plans to continue to prioritize being a wife and mother, while helping produce practical tools to assist homeschool parents and children enjoy and thrive in the process of education.